IMAGES OF ENGLAND

HARWICH AND DOVERCOURT PUBS

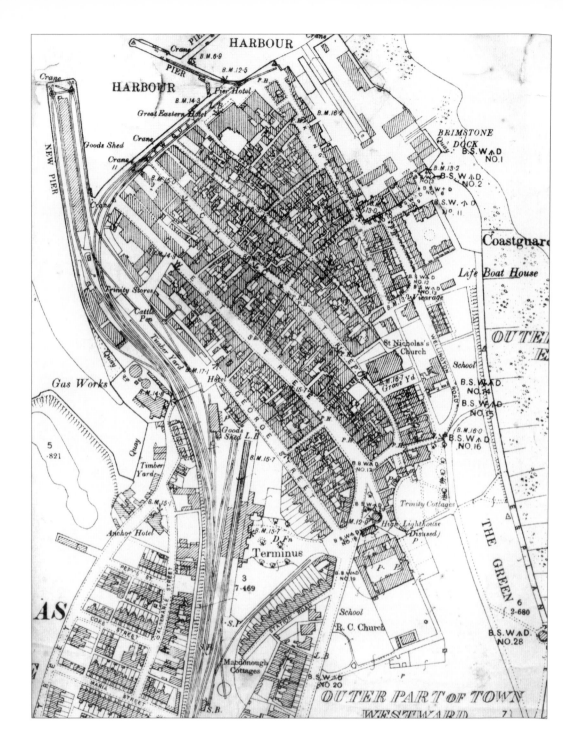

IMAGES OF ENGLAND

HARWICH AND DOVERCOURT PUBS

PETER R. GOODWIN

To Aunt
'The future belongs to those who believe in their dreams'

Frontispiece: Map of Harwich in 1896.

First published 2004

Tempus Publishing Limited
The Mill, Brimscombe Port,
Stroud, Gloucestershire, GL5 2QG
www.tempus-publishing.com

© Peter R. Goodwin, 2004

British Library Cataloguing in Publication Data.
A catalogue record for this book is available from the British Library.

ISBN 0 7524 3309 1

Typesetting and origination by Tempus Publishing Limited.
Printed in Great Britain.

Contents

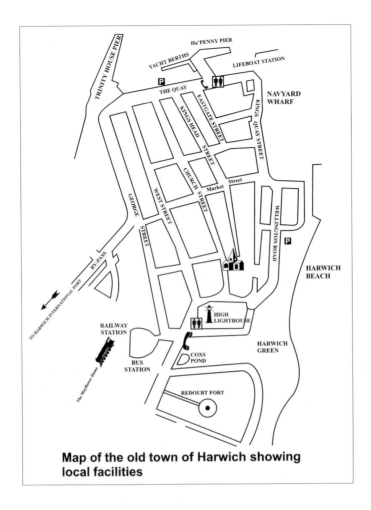

Map of the old town of Harwich showing local facilities

Acknowledgements

To my wife Joy for her support and patience, my daughter Abi – her computer skills being far greater than her dad's – and my sister Jo Booth. I am indebted to John Mowle for his help and advice and Ken Brand for his information and stories found whilst trawling through old newspapers at the Suffolk Record Office. I would like to acknowledge the assistance of the following: Arthur and Peggy Chambers; Mrs Lydia Whitnall; Mrs Beryl Taylor; Bill Turnbull; Brian Knights; Dennis Neal; Brian Smith; Ray Baldry; Philip Cone; Bernie Sadler; Bill Howlett; Mrs Hockley; Mrs Dean; Richard Watts; Pam Colcombe; Sarah Rodger; Janet Thomas; Ivan Hammond; Betty Holbrook; Richard Oxborrow for the Harwich Brewery information and all of the other people who were kind enough to loan me photographs or provide me with useful information.

I am also indebted to Essex Record Office, Suffolk Record Office, Harwich Library, Colchester Library and English Heritage for use of their archives.

Introduction

I have often mulled over in my mind where I got my love of pubs and the hop from, neither my parents nor those of my father were among those who imbibed. My grandfather on my mother's side was a master baker, his father before him a miller, so it was possibly the malt, barley and yeast of the baker's art that has something to do with it.

During the reign of Queen Elizabeth I, so the history books tell, in August of 1561, she 'came hither and accepted of an entertainment from the borough'. On her departure she turned and said, 'A pretty town and wants nothing'.

One wonders if our good queen had frequented the public houses of Harwich, for although in this time there were probably only about four such places, in time the numbers were to grow. It was said that Harwich had more public houses per square mile than any other town, which was probably true of most nautical towns at that time. For instance, Old Gosport boasted, in 1850, sixty such drinking establishments.

In 1604 the borough employed two aletasters and their job was to sample the ale and bread. Such was the quality of the beer and bread that they probably considered themselves to be well employed! In 1666 a Captain Taylor noted that beer was a constant source of trouble, one seldom hearing of good beer. He wrote, 'Here are so many ships and other vessels the charge is so great, it makes me groan to think of it partly occasioned by the bad beer, here is the Wildman whose beer is going the way of all the rest', but as a brewer remarked, 'What could one expect for 3s 6d a cask?' Sea beer was one part strong beer and two parts water. A seaman's allowance was one gallon per day; when one realises the amount of manual work necessary in handling the sails, this was not an excessive quantity. Many will remember a man's allowance swinging a scythe in the harvest fields was eight pints per day.

During the reign of William III, all properties outside of the town wall were passed over to the mayor, aldermen and burgesses of the Harwich Borough Council; this included many of the pubs in the town.

From the early eighteenth century to the start of the twentieth century, the names of almost eighty houses could be named, though not all at one time. Some were the same establishments with the name changed and there were those beer-houses trading from homes that bore no name. A £2 fee to the excise, as no licence was required from the magistrates, was all that sufficed.

With the presence of so many varied occupations and visitors to the town, it was understandable that the number of public houses grew. Present in the town were coastguards, the Royal Navy, merchant seamen, fishermen, army regiments, and later Trinity House, as well as local folk, who all wanted beer, many having their favourite watering holes.

Beer, or ale in the early days (ale was brewed without hops from the middle ages, as hops did not appear in England until the fifteenth century), was brewed as a necessity because the water was not fit for human consumption. Many towns, including Harwich, suffered serious bouts of typhoid. Beer was brewed by farmers and householders alike; even the founder of the Methodist Church, John Wesley, was a brewer, providing safe drinking fluid for his followers, and even children were brought up on beer.

Gin came into being in the 1700s; a far stronger spirit than it is today. If a glass wasn't affordable, a gin-soaked cloth from which to suck the demon spirit was available at a reduced price. In 1913 one poor soul was so desperate that she sold her shoes for gin and in a drunken stupor walked barefoot from Harwich to her home in Parkeston. Arriving at her abode she threatened to kill her children by throwing a lighted oil lamp at them. Her husband restrained her by tying her up while waiting for the police to arrive. She was eventually sent to a home for inebriates.

The Temperance movement had long lobbied for prohibition. As a result, a decree was passed by parliament for local magistrates to reduce the number of pubs by refusing licences.

Public (*publick*) houses had evolved in the seventeenth century from the inns and taverns that abounded in centuries before. The inn was a hostelry wherein the weary traveller could find sustenance and a bed for the night, but with the advent of the steam railway, travellers deserted the horse-drawn coaches and many wayside inns either closed or adapted and became public houses. The tavern was a less grand affair, often being a single room of a dwelling. As a result, the landlord had to supplement his income in other ways – for instance, he became the proverbial 'butcher, baker or candlestick-maker' while his good lady ran the tavern during the day. It was common for many pubs in Harwich to be taken over by ex-seamen and soldiers. The saloon and public bar layout became the fashion during the Victorian era.

At the Brewsters Sessions in 1892, so named because brewing was done in those days of yore by ladies (brewster was the female form of 'brewer'), the Temperance movement started its campaign to reduce the number of pubs in the town. Campaigners objected to the renewal of licence for the Royal Oak, in Market Street, on the grounds that 'there were sufficient other licensed premises in the area, 32 within 200 yards, it having insufficient accommodation, being unfit for habitation and looking at the upper part the windows appeared as though they had seen neither cloth nor water, its appearance being that of a third rate beer house in a low neighbourhood rather than a house of full dignity'. All this in a street that was a busy hub of the town. The bench overrode these objections and granted the renewal.

At the 1894 sessions the movement again objected to licence renewals and the Prince of Wales and Elephant and Castle were at the centre of their objections. The Elephant and Castle had sixteen houses within a 200 yard radius and the Prince of Wales was also in close proximity. It was, however, pointed out that the landlord of the Elephant and Castle had had a long-standing position here (some seventeen years) without trouble. The pub had held a licence for forty years and it was close to the railway station. Referring to the Temperance movement members, the bench declared that they would not refuse a licence on the evidence of 'two rank teetotallers, faddists and miserable objects'.

At the sessions in 1896 it was stated that the number of full licences was thirty-two, beer-houses nine, winesellers four, and convictions for drunkenness thirty-one, while the population of Harwich was 5,089 and Dovercourt 2,710.

The Temperance movement again raised their objections in 1904, this time the Co-operative Society were the centre of their objections, with the London Tavern, which was owned by the society, having its licence up for renewal. Their objection was that 'it adjoined a fully licensed house, the Dukes Head, and that the premises were not structurally fit for the purposes of a licence, with a knot of houses adjoining it and other licensed premises in the near vicinity. Since the society had taken over the house, the premises, which had a 17ft frontage, had been curtailed because the upper storey had been used as a drapery store. The back doors of the grocery shop and the public house were close together and were approached by a join-to passage so that the society, if so disposed, could carry on a liquor business through the shop. As to the class of persons who frequented the place, there was a little box room used as a drinking den by women. On Saturday nights these women could be seen standing outside, waiting their turn to go in. The chairman stated that, with regards to these women, perhaps they were members of the society and might have thought that they were getting something better and purer than elsewhere. He also asked if the objector's wife was a member, since the society had taken over the premises for the benefit of its members; they, of course, paid a dividend. There were 1,200 members of the society who had the right of purchasing their requirements at the Co-operative store and it was thought they should also have the opportunity of buying the beer and spirits there; the store having had 22,000 transactions between 2 October and 22 November the previous year (1903). The London Tavern had held a licence for half a century and had a clean record, but in spite of this the chairman referred to the impending changes in the licensing laws and the bench refused the licence. The renewal of licence saga was to continue for some years to come, with the Royal Oak, New Bell, Prince of Wales and Lifeboat Inn all having their licences reviewed.

Pub signs are part of our history. The first signs, often just a stake, appeared at the taverns beside Roman roads to tempt the weary traveller inside. In 1393 all publicans and brewers were compelled by law to display signs. As few people could read, it was important to have a sign that was eye-catching and distinctive, so some shrewd innkeepers hit on the idea of using heraldic emblems from the local Lords of the Manor; from these evolved the signs that are common today. The Lion evolves from the heraldic symbol of kings, denoting courage and nobleness: the colour would change to suit the monarch. The Red Lion, being the most popular, proclaimed allegiance to John of Gaunt. Henry I was the 'blue king' and Edward IV was the 'white lion'. The end of the Wars of the Roses gave us the Rose & Crown and the Alma derives from the Crimean battle of the Alma.

During the two world wars trade suffered a decline with the closure of more pubs and although things improved during the 1940s, as Harwich was an important naval base and thousands of sailors came ashore after time at sea looking for beer, trade again declined in the 1950s.

Before the days of lager and keg beers, when beer was drawn straight from the barrel, it was the darker beer that bore favour with drinkers – stout always to the fore. With the advent of the handpump, lighter beers, bitter and pale ales gradually became more popular. It is interesting to note that the darker beers are again gaining in popularity amongst lovers of real ale especially in the winter months.

For many years it was possible to buy milk stout until government legislation decreed the word 'milk' must be removed. However, in 1912 the papers reported: 'Considerable attention has lately been directed to Milk Stout, which is a perfect food beverage. Each pint contains the energising carbohydrate of 10oz pure milk. Brewed under licence by Daniel & Sons, West Bergholt (sole licensees for Essex & Suffolk) can be supplied direct from the brewery, or obtained at their houses in Colchester and elsewhere.'

There were a great many brewers in days past that gradually declined over the years. Well-known names, for example, Ind Coope, Daniell & Son, Truman Hanbury and Buxton, Mann Crossman and Paulin disappeared and were taken over by the giant national corporations. Many smaller ones closed for a number of reasons – their identity lost forever – but, as with most things, everything turns full circle, and today there is a new breed of family and micro breweries opening, maintaining the great British tradition of brewing real ale.

As with most towns and villages in recent years, the trends have been for more closures and conversions to housing. Hopefully this trend will cease and public houses will once again become the centre of the communities in which they serve.

We will now start our stroll through Harwich and Dovercourt and see where these pubs were. Each of them has their own tale to tell; some more so than others.

Peter Goodwin
May 2004

one

Harwich

The grand building on the quay, the Great Eastern Hotel, also known as the Harwich Hotel, was built on the site of the old Cock and Pye and was opened by the railway company in 1865. The design, in a 'free Italian or mixed style', was to cater for the prosperous continental traveller, accommodating passengers from the North Sea passenger ships that sailed from the town pier. Such was the elegance of the hotel, many functions were held within its commodious surroundings, one such being Squire Garland's annual dinner in 1896 for his tenants, during which he 'conceded 7½% off their rents'. With the advent of the increased number of ships plying their trade to the continent, the town pier soon outgrew its capacity and a new quay was built at Ray Island, which was then known as Parkeston Quay. The hotel closed its doors in 1910. During the First World War the building became a hospital; then in 1923 the Great Eastern Railway merged with the London and North Eastern Railway, and the new company LNER sold the hotel and other quayside properties by auction in 1936. The hotel was bought by Harwich Corporation and after the Second World War became the Town Hall and magistrates' court. After the changes to local councils, Harwich lost its borough status and became a town council. They then moved the Town Hall to the Guildhall and the hotel was sold and later became apartments and a shipping office.

This period view of Harwich Harbour shows the Great Eastern Hotel and Pier Hotel with one of the steam ships that carried the passengers for the hotels berthed at the town pier.

An advertisement for the Pier Hotel, from 1949.

Alongside the Great Eastern Railway Hotel stands the Pier Hotel, which was built during the 1860s as competition to the railway hotel. Local landlord John Brice purchased the land from the old Harwich Brewery to build his new hotel. Seen in this modern photograph together with the old Angel Inn, which was purchased by the current Pier Hotel owners, the Milsom Group, it now acts as an annexe to the main hotel.

This photograph from around 1906 is interesting in that it shows the original Pier Hotel. Compare this with the modern photograph on page 13 and it can be seen that the rear three bays have been removed. In May 1907 Police Superintendent Ackers reported to the magistrates' bench that 'certain alterations were being carried out without the sanction of the magistrates'. This alteration was apparently made to accommodate storage space. The Yarmouth Arms, also previously known as the Angel and Old Angel, was situated on the quay during the sixteenth century and became a storehouse used by the brewery, which is now the hotel car park. In 1730 the corporation leased to Richard Rolfe part of the quay formally known as Watkins Quay and the public house formerly known as Yarmouth Arms. In 1738 the corporation leased waste ground to the east side of town, a tenement and inn formerly known as the Angel; in 1762, Thomas Cobbold, brewer, leased from the corporation a tenement built on part of the wharf formerly called Watkins Quay. This tenement was known as the Yarmouth Arms and subsequently became known as the Angel and Bell.

Angel Quay from around 1908, showing the Pier Hotel and the Angel Inn. Built in 1824, the Angel was owned by the corporation and leased to Cobbold. It was a popular quayside watering hole until its closure, as can be seen in the above photograph, with sailors and young ladies parading outside along the quay.

The Angel Inn around 1927 with landlord Harry Taylor in the centre of photograph with some of his regulars.

The Angel in the 1950s shows that the door on the corner had been removed and replaced with a window. This pub has now become a free house.

Above: This photograph from the 1960s shows that the Mann's name has been removed from the corner sign, and a road sign has appeared directing the heavy-goods vehicles from the newly opened Navy yard wharf opposite.

Left: Major Kendall's Rolls Royce is seen here outside the Angel in 1962. The major was a flamboyant gentleman who took over the inn around 1954 after leaving the army where he had served since 1915. He joined up at the age of fifteen. After decimalisation, the major would not convert from £sd, refusing to change to 'foreign money at my age'. Ken (the major) retired at the age of seventy-five in 1974.

To the rear of the Angel in Kings Quay Street, or the Slipway as it was previously known, stands the Ship Inn. As with many other buildings this had a previous life in the seventeenth century as a blacksmith's then as a house and became a pub in the mid-1700s. It was then owned, like so many, by the mayor, aldermen and burgesses of the borough corporation. In 1743 the corporation leased to James Clents ground and tenements now used as a public house known as the Bell. The Ship, so it appears, was therefore not its original name. Charrington Nicoll leased it in 1910, but Cobbold took the lease over and finally closed it between the wars around 1927. The photograph seen here is from the early 1950s when the pub became Mrs Roberts second-hand bookshop. Restored by the council in the 1970s, the Ship became a gift shop and then a restaurant as it remains today. In the background can be seen the Duke of Norfolk and Royal Hotel.

The Globe is shown here in the 1960s, adjoining the Ship Inn, the town's oldest surviving pub. It began trading in 1753 when it was owned by Cobbold, who sold it by auction in 1837. Since then, after a short period of closure, it is trading as a popular pub again.

The Plain (Kings Quay Street) is seen here in 1941 and the Globe can be seen in the background.

Another photograph of the Plain, in the 1960s, shows the former Jolly Sailor that was owned in 1827 by Samuel John Self. It was later taken over by his son John and became a hardware shop. Today it trades as the Bear restaurant.

A modern day photograph of the Bear with the Globe in the background.

John Self's shop, the former Jolly Sailor, is seen here around 1910. Opposite is the old Duke of Norfolk. It is thought that the Duke of Norfolk was on the same site as the Privateer. Reputedly once the Palace of the Duke of Norfolk, it was built by Cobbold in the 1850s and closed around the time of the First World War. It was demolished as part of the Harwich redevelopment scheme and is now council flats.

Left: Looking down the quaint St Austins Lane, stands the Half Moon, in Eastgate Street, which was another Cobbold house. It was trading in 1753, sold by auction in 1837 by Thomas Cobbold and taken up by Nathaniel Cobbold, who sold it on to the Colchester Brewing Company. The pub closed in the 1960s and became an antique shop and today it is a private dwelling. In 1899 the landlord William Dowling, aged fifty-nine, died suddenly having been unwell for five months, but Dr Evans, who had attended him medically, refused to give a death certificate. Inspector Fulcher communicated with the coroner, Dr Harrison, explaining every particular in full. Dr Harrison then considered an inquest necessary. The deceased lived in Harwich for many years, and was a pensioner from the Royal Navy and had served in the Crimean War.

Looking up St Austins Lane from the corner of Eastgate Street, this photograph shows a different view of the Half Moon before the area was destroyed. Landlord William Jessop of the Half Moon pleaded guilty in 1902 to having harboured 1¾ lbs of tobacco upon which no duty had been paid. He was ordered to pay double the value and duty amounting to 18s 8d with costs of 9s 6d, or 14 days hard labour. The defendant paid the money.

The Colchester Brewing Company, on 17 July 1907, applied for temporary transfer of the licence on the grounds that the tenant had moved from the premises. On 19 June he left the house without saying anything to his wife. The following day she received a letter with a Liverpool postmark, with certain accounts which he alleged were due to him from certain customers. There could be little doubt that he had gone to America.

In 1909 the body of Benjamin Colthorpe, landlord of the Half Moon, was found in the dykes near the Old Smack; he had had financial problems. The inquest verdict was suicide while suffering temporary insanity.

Right: The Wild Boar, No. 16 Kings Quay Street, was situated between the Duke of Norfolk and the Wellington Inn. It was trading in 1870 but is now demolished and forms part of the council flats. The start of demolition and destruction can be seen in this photograph from around 1952, which shows part of the area of Red Lion Yard where the Red Lion once stood. The top left-hand corner shows where the Duke of Norfolk would have stood and also the rear of the Wild Boar.

Below: This 1960s view of the same area being demolished shows the site where the Duke of Norfolk, Wild Boar and the Red Lion would have stood. The rear of the Wellington Inn can also be seen.

The Duke of Wellington, No. 18 Kings Quay Street, is seen here around 1960. It had seen better times but was still trading then and was known to have been trading in 1845 when it was a former Tolly Cobbold pub. Plans were submitted in 1897 to alter the premises; one room was to become a music hall and permission was granted under the Amended Public Health Act, which gave power to any publican to use a portion of his premises as a music hall. The premises, No. 16 Kings Quay Street, two doors down where the boarded-up shops are, would have been the Wild Boar. In the bankruptcy case on 2 August 1907 of Messrs Smith and Beaumont (Harwich builders), Messrs Craske & Sons offered the fully licensed house, the Wellington and other freehold properties, for sale at the Three Cups Hotel, Harwich. There was a good attendance of gentlemen from the town and district. The following prices were obtained. The fully licensed public house, the Wellington, let to Mr J.D. Cobbold at £125 a year, and occupied by Mr Stanley Greenwood. The other properties offered were not licensed premises. At this time, 1907-25, it is shown that the landlord was a Frank Greenwood who was a tenant for Cobbold. The 'Welly' is now residential properties.

An advertisement for the Wellington Inn from a 1950s edition of the *Harwich and Dovercourt Official Handbook*.

Mark Stansall welcomes you to

" The New Bell " (SEE MAP OVER)

HARWICH 3545   WELLINGTON RD., HARWICH
SNACKS & SANDWICHES ALWAYS AVAILABLE
Fully licensed **FREE** house . **HEINEKEN** draught lager

Above left: The New Bell Inn situated in Outpart Eastward, was originally a blacksmith's from 1620 through to 1743 when the building had a change of use and was converted to a pub. It was then originally known as the Bell, however, the pub was owned by the corporation and the collector of dues, in order to avoid confusion with the Blue Bell further down the same road, wrote in his book 'New Bell'. The name was then officially changed to the New Bell. In 1908 the New Bell had an annual turnover of 150-180 barrels of beer and 150 gallons of spirits. Originally a Grays of Chelmsford pub, it became a Mann's pub in 1910, the fourth Mann Crossman and Paulin pub in Harwich. In 1982 the lease of the pub was taken by Mr and Mrs Colcomb and the freehold was bought from the council in 1988. In 1883 the landlord, one William Pearce, was charged and convicted (although he produced a card displayed behind the bar showing that all spirits were sold diluted with water), of selling adulterated gin which was cut with 60 per cent water and fined £1 or 14 days' hard labour. Mr Pearce also applied for an hour's extension for a smoking concert and, in 1889, permission for this was granted. These smoking concerts were popular events in those days. 'Marine's terrible death' was the newspaper headline on 16 November 1905. A Royal Marine from HMS *Boscawen II* entered the New Bell and asked for refreshment. As he was worse for drink the landlord, Mr Walsh, refused to serve him. The marine then went away but appeared shortly after. By this time the house was closed and as his knocks were being ignored he broke a panel of glass on the door. The landlord ran for the police, but the marine took off his coat, ran across the road and took a flying leap through the plate glass windows. Bleeding profusely, he staggered behind the bar, and was found smothered with blood – the main artery of his arm had been severed. Dr Reynolds was called and the man was transferred to the Naval sick quarters, where he died from exhaustion.

Above right: The New Bell in 2004, which trades today as a free house and is popular with real ale drinkers. It gained entry into the Camra *Good Beer Guide* 2005. Adjacent to the New Bell are Bell Cottages. The Blue Bell was also in Outpart Eastward, a beer-house that was owned by Alston's the brewers of Manningtree between 1870 and 1885 and whose charwoman was Sarah Wink. The Blue Bell was sold in 1919 and demolished to make way for cottages. In 1875 local mariners, Matthew Scarlett, James Wink and John Kedge were charged with assaulting Pte Henry Ling of the 96th Regiment of Foot. One of the defendants, without provocation, struck Pte Ling with his fist and knocked him out and the other two started kicking him. The landlord dismissed all four from the pub. The magistrates fined Wink 5s and 15s costs. Scarlett and Kedge were both fined 20s and 10s costs.

The Brewery Tap, owned by John Chevalier Cobbold between 1873 and 1880, is shown as a beer-house in Outpart Eastward. It is likely that this was part of the brewery at the rear of St Nicholas church and the Three Cups.

This 1969 photograph, with Betty Holbrook watching on, shows the demolition of the Royal Hotel, which stood in Wellington Road and fronted the Market Place (also shown here in Outpart Eastward), and No. 43 Kings Quay Street, an ale-house in 1866 that was owned by Cobbold. In 1898 the newspaper reported that the hotel was under the sole management of Mr and Mrs Bernard Asplen: 'it has been recently redecorated and upholstered throughout, now being replete with every hotel convenience, bids fair to become one of the most popular houses in the district'. The Royal was sold by Cobbold in 1927 and became the Royal Flats. Cobbold made the promise to build a new Royal in Dovercourt as a replacement. The site is now a greensward.

Opposite below: Bearing left into Kings Head Street, known by locals as Dirty Street, on the far right of this 1956 photograph (which was before these buildings were demolished), shows premises that could have been the Prince of Orange, which was shown to have been in this part of the street. Opposite the Prince of Orange, on the corner of the street, stood the Lifeboat Inn, known prior to 1877 as the Red, White and Blue. It was owned by the Cobbolds until 1879 when it was sold by auction to Charrington Nicoll for £640. At the renewal of licensing in 1880, the turnover was said to be 156 barrels per year, and was referred to as 'the house … bad for the supervision of the police and the landlord, the class of people using the house comprised pedlars, tramps, rag and bone dealers, organ grinders etc.,'. The Lifeboat was demolished during the 1950s as part of the redevelopment scheme in Area No. 1.

Above: Moving into Market Street, the Kings Head, which would have been on the far right of this busy street, is shown in the parish records of 1612-97 as the Kings Head plus dwelling house. It was known as the house of the dancing bears – seamen bringing bears ashore to dance in the pub – and had eight lodging rooms and no cellar. It was owned by Thomas Cobbold from 1753, who sold it by auction in 1837 to J.F.P & A.T Osborne. In 1875 a meeting was held in the pub for the purpose of considering what steps should be taken to organise a Cooperative store in the town, for some reason 'employees of the Great Eastern Railway mustered in large numbers'. The pub suffered a fire in the same year, landlord Mr Last being woken by a strong smell; a mat in front of the fire had ignited. Mr Last extinguished the fire and was compensated for the damage by his insurance company. Whilst in the ownership of the Colchester Brewing Company, the Kings Head, like many pubs suffering loss of trade due to the departure of the Army and Navy, fell into disuse. The last landlord was Mr Lodge, who sold it to Mr Leonard Rose in the 1930s, after which it was converted to the Labour Exchange, or 'Dole Office', the mahogany bar making an excellent counter, and sufficient rooms to provide accomodation for a caretaker/cleaner. Today, the building is Bill Howlett's General Store.

The Lifeboat Inn and adjoining properties before their demolition in the 1950s.

The Lion Inn stood in East Street sometime between 1726 and 1819 after which time the property became a tenement dwelling and 'bake office'. When the street was renamed it became No. 11 Kings Head Street and was owned until 1901 by a baker, Jonathan Brewster. At No. 14 stood the Swan Inn, shown in the photograph from 1921 as Swan Stores and is in an advanced state of dereliction. It was previously known as the Bell and Dragon and around the eighteenth century, as the Ship. George Imray, a seaman aboard HMS *Eagle* that was lying in the harbour in 1891, was convicted of stealing four forks and a knife value 2s 6d, belonging to the landlord Edward Long. Imray was fined 5s and costs of 11s.

The Swan over the past years has been renovated and is now a private dwelling as can be seen from this photograph taken in 2004.

Across the road at No. 28 the Alma Inn was once a merchant's house or mansion owned by Captain Twitt, a relative of Thomas Twytt, a merchant and brewer of Harwich in 1599. The Alma traded as an alehouse around 1873 and was owned by Charles Cunningham, a brewer of Ipswich. It then became a Tolly Cobbold house (popular with local fishermen) and the tenant, from 1932 until 1953, was William Chambers. Upon his retirement the tenancy was taken up by his son Arthur who ran it until 1987. Today the fine etched windows can still be seen. This photograph from 1932 outside the pub shows, from left to right: Tom Brewster; Rosie Hendrick; Harry Holden; Harry Holden's dad; Mrs Tilly; Mrs Bloomfield; Bill Chambers; landlord; Alice McClelland; landlady Mrs Chambers; Mrs Warner; Alice Dale; Len Edwards Mrs Bright with the hat; and in the front row Laura Hendrick and Rosie Dale.

The Alma as it is today. After the closure of the Tolly Cobbold Brewery the Alma, along with the majority of the Tolly pubs, was taken over by Pubmaster, who in turn were bought by Punch Taverns in 2004.

Taking the cut through Hopkins Lane, brings us out into Church Street, where at No. 31, stands the Rose and Crown; an eighteenth-century front on an earlier timber-framed house. It later became a shop and fishmongers. Today, as the photograph depicts, it has been restored and trades as the Samuel Pepys, better known as 'Sam's Wine Bar'.

Right: The Fleur de Lys, which had a Elizabethan courtyard and is now known as Cobbolds Court, was once Cobbolds Yard and sold in 1911 for the purpose of erecting a well-equipped Naval sailors' home. It was formerly (during the period 1658-1746) known as the Tabbard later becoming the Dolphin. It was sold in 1742 by Abraham Groom to Thomas Cobbold who later sold it on to Georgio Rolfe and again on to John Rolfe of the Rolfe brewing family. The site now is occupied by Mayflower House. Continuing up Church Street just round the corner at No. 22 Market Street stands the Royal Oak. This modern photograph shows a restored façade of a building that was not known for its hygiene in days past. On 11 September 1757 John Smith leased the pub to Thomas Cobbold for 5s. The pub in turn was rented to the occupant Mary Young the widow, for one peppercorn. In 1908 it had a turnover of 180 barrels and 80 gallons of spirits per annum. The Royal Oak is now a private dwelling.

Below: An advertisement for the Duke's Head Inn from the 1950s.

Duke's Head Inn = Harwich

Prop. W. F. Ingram

TELEPHONE 747

(A comfortable 16th Century Inn)

COACHES WELCOME

BED & BREAKFAST

MUSIC

SNACKS

Roomy Bars
Cheery Atmosphere

Fully
Licensed

Cosy Lounge
Good Service

Above: On the corner of Currants Lane, at No. 22 Church Street, the Duke's Head was known as a dwelling in 1632. In 1885 the landlord, Charles Burroughs, fell down the steps to his cellar and received injuries from which he died. The inquest verdict was accidental death due to a fracture at the base of the skull.

Right above: The Wheatsheaf, formerly the Co-op Tavern, was built to replace the London Tavern, and included the Co-op confectionary shop. Shown to have been owned by the Harwich & Dovercourt Industrial Co-operative Society from 1910, it was 'Divi with your beer', the Co-op giving its members a dividend with their beer, many members keeping their 'divi' until Christmas when they could buy the bottles of beer for the festive period. Sold in 1960, it was renamed the Stingray and is still trading today.

Right below: The Bear, later known as the King's Arms, was purchased by the Corporation of Harwich in 1673 and converted to the Guildhall and Gaol. In 1769 it was rebuilt and enlarged as it is seen today. The *Ipswich Journal* of May 1753 reported that 'to be seen at the King's Arms, the surprising dancing bears, late arrived from abroad, who by infinite deal of labour and trouble are brought to foot by violin, both in comic dances and hornpipes, even beyond imagination. The largest of them all is eight feet tall, and dances to the admiration of all beholders. They have had the honour twice to perform before His Majesty King George, his Royal Highness the Prince of Wales, the Duke of Cumberland, and upwards of 300 of the nobility in London. They perform many other particulars as expressed in the bills, and are separated by a partition; the gentlemen and ladies may see their performances without fear'. Today the Guildhall is the home of the Harwich Town Council, and houses the town archives.

Opposite below: Next door to the Duke's Head at No. 21 stands the London Tavern. It was owned from 1870 until 1878 by the trustees of John Pattrick (deceased, Dovercourt) and traded as an ale-house. It was purchased by the Co-operative Society, who ran it as a pub and also a drapery store. In 1895 the landlord, John Osborne, while returning from a drive in his trap, collided with a gentleman on his safety cycle. The trap was overturned, Mr Osborne was thrown out and received a severe shaking, while the bicycle was smashed and its rider severely cut about the hands and face. Poor Mr Osborne was in trouble again in 1902. Summonsed for allowing his chimney to become fired and fined 2s 6d. It appears Mr Osborne's chimney became fired again in 1911, as a fire broke out in the drapery department upstairs caused (it is thought) by a large wooden beam becoming overheated and igniting. The fire was extinguished and a considerable amount of damage was caused. It was fortunate that the fire was discovered prior to closing time, otherwise an outbreak of far greater proportions would have occurred. Shortly after this episode, the Co-operative Society decided to close the pub and build a new one opposite and converted the tavern completely to a drapers. The building interior was destroyed by fire in 1952, and is now a private dwelling.

The Three Cups at No. 64 Church Street, an inn and posting house, was an Elizabethan mansion and purpose-built hostelry built in the sixteenth century and constructed of ships' timbers. An extra wing was added in the seventeenth century and the top storey was removed in 1949. Sir James Thornhill says in his diary of 1711, 'Sun 3 June dined at ye 3 Cupps'.

The death was announced, at about midday on 27 February 1875, of Mr Joseph Leech Bull, landlord of the Three Cups and farmer of Blue House Farm. The deceased was an old and highly respected inhabitant. The licence was transferred to John Bull whose son William was to become brewer at the 'workhouse brewery'.

Right: The Three Cups was a highly popular establishment, and many organisations held functions there, such as in 1901 the Annual Dinner of the Harwich railway station staff, and in 1904 the Police Subscription Dinner. Nevertheless, they did have problems: in 1901 Mr Bray, the landlord, was charged with permitting his house to be used as a resort for persons of ill repute – these persons being ladies of the night. The case, after evidence was submitted, was dismissed.

Below: The newspaper reported in October 1892 that the clematis tree at the Three Cups was, according to annual custom, prettily decorated with fairy lamps and Chinese lanterns. The tree was planted by Mrs Bull in 1851 and covered the whole of the courtyard. The Cups is now a private dwelling.

BOTTLED ALES AND STOUT

SINGLE BOTTLES SUPPLIED.

When ordering Ale, ask for "TOLLY"
When ordering Stout, ask for "BEANO" Stout

					¼-Bots.	Per doz. Bots.	Flagons.
"Tolly" Ales.							
Light Bitter Brown Ale Double Stout }	-	-	-	-	-	**4/-**	**7/-**	**13/-**
Light Tolly Dark Tolly }	-	-	-	.	.	**4/6**	**8/-**	—
"Beano" Stout	-	-	-	.	.	**4/6**	**8/-**	**16/-**

FREMLIN'S

"E.B."

ELEPHANT BRAND ALE

BITTERED ENTIRELY WITH HOPS

For list of prices, see page 28.

Above: It has always been reputed that Nelson's Room in the Three Cups was where Lord Nelson stayed with Lady Hamilton on a visit to Harwich. This story holds not a thread of truth as Nelson remained on board his ship HMS *Medusa* in 1801 while it was lying in Harwich harbour. This may have been wishful thinking on Lady Hamilton's part, but is difficult as she hadn't made the journey to visit him.

Left: An advertisement for Tolly Ales and Stout from John Buckle of Kensington, Wine Merchant, Price List.

An advertisement for the Hanover Inn in Church Street.

The Hanover Inn, No. 65 Church Street, shown as it is today, was previously known as the Hanover Square Rooms. Advertised in 1858 as an 'eating house also providing well-aired beds', in 1872 the Hanover dining rooms were licensed as a beer-house and became known as an inn. In 1888 the rooms had a narrow escape when a paraffin lamp suspended to a beam in the dining room fell on to a table and broke, setting fire to the table cloth, carpets and rugs. But for the prompt and praiseworthy actions of Mrs Lawrence and her daughter, a serious fire would have occurred. The house, no doubt, would have been destroyed. Mrs Lawrence's clothing caught fire, but happily she escaped injury. Thankfully, Mr Lawrence was insured. Mr William Lawrence the landlord retired in 1910 and moved to Albermarle Street. He had been badly gored by one of his prize bulls that he grazed on land near the Redoubt with his dairy cows. It appears he was a tyrant to his sons but much loved by his spinster daughters, this according to his great-great-granddaughter. William died in March 1928 at the age of ninety-two. A visitor, the Hon. Hugh de Wac, was convicted in 1892 of stealing a watch, valued at £1, the property of Miss Minnie Lawrence. He was sentenced to one month's hard labour. In 1958 owner Cobbold united with Tollemache and the Hanover became fully licensed.

Above: An interior photograph of the bar in the Foresters Arms.

Opposite: The Foresters Arms stands opposite the Hanover in Hanover Square, at No. 5 Church Street, and was built around 1450. Three generations of the Barwood family kept the pub until 1942 when, damaged by incendiaries during the war, the pub closed and although it was not inhabited it was still furnished. Mr Barwood retained the keys and visited it on a daily basis. When he passed away, his daughter, who was managing the Golden Lion, was offered the Foresters by Ind Coope. On declining their offer, Ind Coope declared it would never open again as a pub and sold the property. The pub was sold to Mrs Winifred Cooper who restored the building and lived in it until she passed away. It is now the headquarters of the Harwich Society. It was nicknamed the 'Old Drum and Monkey'. The name is believed to have derived from either a drum hanging from the ceiling that a monkey would bang on to warn of a customer or the licensee would send the monkey round for a penny in the drum when bad language was used. In 1884 landlord Daniel Barwood was among a gang of men at Wrabness unloading the Swedish barque *Augusta* laden with timber. Daniel was engaged at the winch, and while heaving up a load of timber, the ratchet or catch of the windlass broke. The handle revolved at great speed striking him across the forehead and smashing in the bone causing a wound of 3 inches in length and 1½ inches in depth. He was removed to his home and attended by Dr Evans. The poor fellow lay in a dangerous condition but was expected to recover. (Reproduced by kind permission of English Heritage)

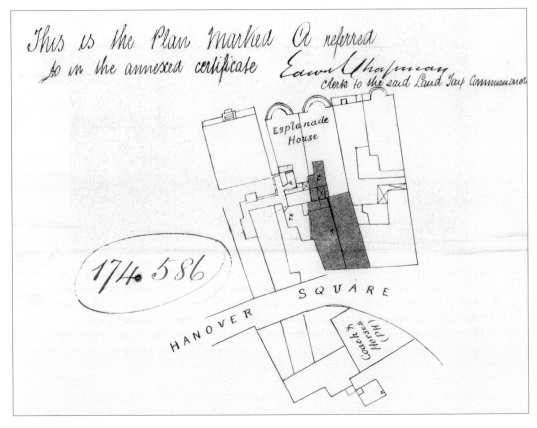

This is the Plan marked A referred to in the annexed certificate Edwin Chapman Clerks to the said Land Tax Commissioner

Esplanade House

174. 586

HANOVER SQUARE

Coach & Horses (H.P.H.)

Above: Hanover Square evolved from local MP John Robinson, who in the late eighteenth century promised to 'remove the great inconveniences which arose from the narrowness of the highway and approach leading from West Street to Saint Helen's and Church Streets', by demolishing old properties and widening the road. The plan doesn't show the Hanover Inn but does show the Coach and Horses. Hanover Square became part of Church Street in the late nineteenth century.

Left: An advertisement for the Coach & Horses.

The Coach and Horses, Hanover Square, No. 2 Church Street, was later known as the Bull and is shown here in the early 1900s with the choir boys from St Nicholas church parading by. Today it is a showroom for Harwich Radio and Cycle Supplies. The newspaper reported in May 1889 that, 'the body of Mrs Goodwin, wife of Mr Goodwin, late of the Coach and Horses, was found ashore on Stone Point. A bunch of keys with her initials on putting identification beyond all doubt. It is just a month since the poor woman was reported missing, money and a gold watch reported to be on her person were not found.' Another report from 1 January 1902 stated: 'A boy aged 15, on the 1 January 1902, the son of an employee of the Harwich Gas and Coke Company was discovered hanging by a rope in an out house adjoining the Coach and Horses, where it was said he had been employed as an ostler. Doctor Welch certified that life was extinct; the body was removed to the mortuary.'

Turning into West Street, at No. 14 is the Six Bells (built *c.* 1800). It was later to become a bakery and the business was owned by Mr Carter who baked bread for the Co-operative Society. The bakery workers shown in this photograph are seen here from around 1915. After the Co-operative Society had moved to their own bakery, the shop became a greengrocers. Upon the owner's death, Mr Humphries opened it again as a bakery, as it remained until closure in 2004.

Across the road at No. 74 West Street was the Spread Eagle, shown here in 1951. During the period 1684 to 1870 it was known as the Star. Formerly a Cobbold house, it was later taken by Ind Coope as an ale-house. It was reported in 1893 that a fifteen-year-old girl, Florence Pettit, the youngest daughter of Mrs Tovell, had been taken seriously ill at about 10 p.m., and died at 2 a.m. the following day. The deceased had always been a delicate girl. On Sunday she appeared in her usual health and on returning from the church assisted in the bar until closing time. After supper Mrs Tovell, seeing that the deceased was looking very ill, sent for a doctor, who advised that she should be put to bed and kept very quiet; shortly afterwards she became worse. The doctor was sent for again, but in the short time elapsing before his arrival, she died. Mrs Tovell was the landlady, having had the licence transferred to her from her husband since he had deserted her in 1887, and she had not heard from him for three years.

THE "SPREAD EAGLE"

HARWICH.

Proprietor: W. INGRAM.

Commercial Hotel.

FINEST WINES, SPIRITS AND BEERS.   MOTOR GARAGE.
BILLIARDS.   HORSES AND TRAPS FOR HIRE.

Bottled Ales and Stouts delivered to any part of the district.

Headquarters of Harwich and Parkeston Football Club.

Try our noted Bottled Beers, Bass, Guiness, &c.
Accommodation for Parties.

A public meeting held at the Spread Eagle on 6 February 1922 resulted in £500 being handed over in under ten minutes. This was the amount that Harwich & Parkeston FC required to purchase the Royal Oak ground. It was proudly claimed that the borough was assured of a football venue for perpetuity.

Above: The Elephant and Castle, No. 11 West Street, shown here in 1950, was previously the Welcome Sailor. In 1896 Tollemache Bros, brewers, made an application to rebuild the pub, as it was in a very dilapidated condition. The plans show that they intended to purchase two cottages, one in West Street the other in Golden Lion Lane and that the costs of the improvements would be around £1,000. The mayor remarked that it would be a 'decided public improvement', the permission was granted and the new pub was built in 1904. The pub later changed its name to the Haywain and then in 2002 to the Mariners.

Right: The Prince of Wales, No. 18 West Street, shown here in its present form as private dwellings, was an eighteenth-century red-brick house, although records show it to be trading during the period 1684 to 1870. At the sessions in 1894 application was made for the transfer of its licence to William Smy. Superintendent Ackers objected on the ground that Smy had been convicted at Ipswich in 1893 for having permitted riotous behaviour in a house he then occupied. The Prince of Wales closed in 1908 when it was combined with another property to form flats.

An advertisement for the Duke of Edinburgh from the early 1950s.

The Duke of Edinburgh, seen here in the 1960s, stands at No. 65 West Street and trades today as the Billy. Anthony Cox leased the pub, originally known as the Harwich Arms, to Thomas Cobbold in 1824. The indenture showed it to be the Harwich Arms, shop and yard in West Street. Thomas Cobbold bought the pub in 1753, selling it to Nathaniel Cobbold in 1837 and it was later taken over by the Colchester Brewing Company. By then the name had changed to the King William the Fourth in around 1870 and then to the Duke of Edinburgh. The papers reported in 1876 that, 'a bull being driven to the railway trucks with other beasts strayed from the path of rectitude laid out for him by the drovers and scampered up West Street. Whether it was the jovial looking picture of King William the Fourth which gracefully swings over the door over one of the temples of Bacchus known by that appelation, or whether it may have been the inviting odour of certain stimulants which are kept inside, is a matter open to discussion, but whatever the cause the fascination may have arisen, the bull, without further ado, betook himself straightaway in through the front door, until even his tail was lost from view. The uninitiated were soon acquainted with the facts by a crowd of urchins in the street. The drovers and a crowd of foresaid urchins ensuring the bull retraced his steps until he reached the cattle pens where several female friends tendered their congratulations to him'.

Right: The British Flag, No. 57a West Street, shown here in 1889 when it was owned by F. Kettle and the brewers were Woods & Co. of Colchester. Frederick Kettle, who had the British Flag from 1881 to 1898, started his mineral water business in the cellar before moving to Gwynne Road in Dovercourt. Standing outside the British Flag are the Kettles family. In 1907, when Ernest Knights was landlord, two labourers of 'no fixed abode' were charged with wilful damage to a plate glass window. The men had gone to the police station asking for a bed for the night. When refused, they said 'Well lock us up, we have thrown a chisel through a window in Golden Lion Lane.' When the police found their story was correct, the men were apprehended. They pleaded that they had no money, were hungry and wanted lodgings. The magistrate accommodated them by sentencing them to fourteen days' hard labour.

The British Flag in 1930. Mr Stevens, who was grandfather to Mrs Lydia Whitnall, took the licence in 1911 when it was Mann & Co., a beer-house, until 1953 when the brewery obtained a full licence from the Harwich court, which cost £2,000. The British Flag was the first Mann, Crossman & Paulin house in Harwich. The pub was always a popular house with Trinity House seamen. Mr and Mrs Whitnall were landlords for fifty years taking over from Mrs Whitnall's parents Mr and Mrs Tootell who had been landlords from 1923 until their retirement. They can be seen in this photograph standing outside the British Flag in 1927.

The British Flag is seen here in 1927 and the young lady is Lydia Whitnall with her parents Mr and Mrs Tootell. Also in the photograph is Bill Mayes.

The British Flag again in 1927. Among those standing outside are: Ivy Dyer, daughter of the Duke's Head landlord; Harry Harrison the wood grainer; Ethel Upson; and Mr and Mrs Tootell.

Above: The British Flag in 1927 showing the superb wood-graining carried out by Harry Harrison either side of the doors to the public bar, bottles and jugs and smoke room.

Right: A later, probably 1960s, photograph of the British Flag after the wood-graining has been removed. This was done by order of the Norwich Brewery some years before.

The Packet Inn, No. 72 West Street, was converted from a Georgian house and in 1836 the address was shown as Custom House Lane. It was previously known as the Smack (*Minutes of the Court of Common Council,* 1782) and Eagle Pacquet Boat. In 1919 the landlord, Mr Gloster, and Emily Sealey employed a cleaner and general help, Hilda Cooper, who was reputed to have the cleanest scrubbed tables of any pub in Harwich. Photographed here in 2004, the Packet has reverted to being a house.

Returning up West Street and cutting through Golden Lion Lane brings us to the Golden Lion, at Nos 17-18 George Street. In 1873 it was a beer-house owned by J.F.P. and A.T. Osborne and was taken over in 1910 by the Colchester Brewing Company, then post-1925, by Ind Coope. It was granted a full licence in 1952. In 1942 Mr and Mrs Dean managed the pub and were paid £2 10s per week with a 2s 6d drink allowance. In 1891 the *Harwich Steam* lifeboat rescued the crew from the three-masted schooner *Mercury* bound from Grangemouth to Buenos Aires laden with coal. The vessel had run aground on the Longsand and the crew were taken to Harwich where 'they received every attention from Mr Martin of the Golden Lion'. It became Blazers in the early 1980s when all of the photographs and mementoes adorning the walls were destroyed. Renamed yet again as the Smugglers for a while, it is now almost back to its original name, being called the Lion, as in this 2004 photograph.

The Valuable Freehold Premises

FORMERLY KNOWN AS

THE RAILWAY TAVERN

George Street, Harwich

Well situate in George Street, to which it possesses
a valuable frontage of about 29ft. 4in. Close
to the Quay and Railway Station.

The property is substantially built in brick with a slated
roof (pantiled roof to Kitchen) and contains the following
accommodation :

On the Ground Floor :

ENTRANCE PASSAGE.

PUBLIC BAR (23ft. by 15ft. 6in.) with Tortoise stove.

BAR PARLOUR (15ft. by 7ft. 11in.) with barless grate.

BACK LOBBY.

PRIVATE BAR (11ft. by 8ft. 10in.) with barless grate.

LIVING ROOM (16ft. by 13ft. 2in.) with barless grate.

KITCHEN (19ft. 6in. by 18ft.) with range, sink (cold over),
    point for gas cooker, fitted cupboards and shelves.

LARDER (9ft. 2in. by 8ft. 7in.).

COAL STORE.

LARGE CELLAR beneath the Public Bar.

On the First Floor :

LANDING with cupboard and fireplace.

CLUB ROOM (40ft. 8in. by 19ft.) with two fireplaces and two
    doors.

FRONT ROOM (14ft. by 8ft. 5in.) with fireplace, divided from
    Club Room by a screen.

W.C.

On the Second Floor :

LANDING with two cupboards.

FRONT BEDROOM No. 1 (17ft. by 8ft. 5in.) with fireplace.

FRONT BEDROOM No. 2 (17ft. by 9ft.).

FRONT BEDROOM No. 3 (17ft. by 9ft.) with fireplace.

" L " SHAPED BEDROOM No. 4 (9ft. by 8ft. 5in. overall).

BACK BEDROOM No. 5 (15ft. by 11ft. 5in.) with fireplace.

BACK BEDROOM No. 6 (13ft. by 11ft. 3in.) with fireplace.

Outside :

Brick and pantiled WASHHOUSE AND STORE with brick copper
    and range.

Concreted YARD.

URINAL.

W.C.

Sale details for the Railway Tavern from 17 September 1952.

The Valuable Freehold Premises

FORMERLY KNOWN AS

THE LITTLE EASTERN

George Street, Harwich

Situate immediately adjoining Lot One and possessing a valuable frontage of 17ft. 6in. to George Street.

The property is substantially built in brick with a slated roof and contains the following accommodation :

On the Ground Floor :

ENTRANCE PASSAGE.

PUBLIC BAR (17ft. 10in. by 12ft. 7in.) with brick fireplace.

BAR PARLOUR (13ft. 11in. by 9ft. 1in.) with barless grate and tiled surround, cupboard in recess.

LARGE CELLAR beneath the bars.

On the First Floor :

LANDING.

KITCHEN (17ft. 9in. by 12ft. 3in. widest measurement) with sink (cold over) and range.

LIVING ROOM (16ft. 3in. by 12ft. 4in.) with barless grate and glazed cupboard.

On the Second Floor :

LANDING with cupboard.

FRONT BEDROOM (15ft. 10in. by 12ft. 3in.) with fireplace, cupboard and shelves in recess.

BACK BEDROOM (17ft. 9in. by 12ft. 3in.) with fireplace and cupboard.

BOX ROOM.

Outside :

Concreted YARD.

URINAL.

TWO W.C.'s.

The small Garden is not the property of the Vendor but is rented at £5 per annum and the benefit of the tenancy will be assigned to the purchaser.

The property is offered with

VACANT POSSESSION

on completion of the purchase

Sale details for the Little Eastern from 17 September 1952.

The Little Eastern, No. 11 George Street, was a beer-house, owned in 1873 by Bridges & Co., brewers of Ipswich. It was later to be taken over by the Colchester Brewing Company. The licence was surrendered in 1952 and the pub was demolished along with the White Hart and the Railway Tavern to make way for a residential area. On 25 January 1894, the death of Mr Henry Tyrell Dawson, senior partner of Messrs. Smith, Beaumont and Dawson (builders and contractors of Harwich) and landlord of the Little Eastern Inn occurred. Mr Tyrell was sixty-three years of age and he was also the oldest licensed victualler in the borough. The landlords of both the Little Eastern and the Railway Tavern had applied for a full licence in 1877 on the grounds that a large number of visitors experienced inconvenience from not being able to obtain spirits. Both houses had been conducted in an orderly manner and spirit was used more as a medicine than an intoxicant. Stout and beer were what was termed as 'heavy wet', and people might get drunk just as soon as drinking them as by taking spirits. The magistrates refused the application.

The Railway Tavern, at No. 10 George Street, was trading in the late eighteenth century as a Beer House and was owned from 1873 through to 1952 by Charrington Nicoll. On the evening of Tuesday 26 April 1894 a few friends met at the Railway Tavern, by invitation of Mr and Mrs Salter, to pass a pleasant evening. Advantage was taken to present a very handsome marble clock with bronze side figures to Mr Salter and a handsome gold bracelet to Mrs Salter. Both were suitably engraved with inscriptions stating that the presents were from a few old friends in remembrance of the many kindnesses received at the hands of the host and hostess. On the evening of Thursday 15 May 1897 a very successful smoking concert, under the auspices of the 1st Essex Harwich Artillery Volunteers, was held with the purpose of presenting ex-bandmaster C.R. Salter with a testimonial which consisted of a silver tea and coffee set. The funeral of landlord Charles R Salter took place on Tuesday 30 August 1897. Mourners included Mr R.H. Salter (nephew) and Mrs R.H. Salter.

Opposite below: The White Hart is seen here before closure. Alongside the pub in White Hart Lane is the Mission to Seamen and the Seaman's Pool Office and on the far corner Flood's shop. The pub was sold in 1954 and became Lansbury House, headquarters of the Labour Party.

No. 3 George Street, the White Hart inn and posting house, was trading back at least to 1791 and was sold in 1833 as part of the St Botolph Brewery of Colchester's estate. It was also known as the Railway Hotel. It was described in the *Eastern Counties Business Review* of 1890 as being a 'family and commercial hotel, and one of the very best in Harwich. It is one of the oldest, dating back in history for more than two hundred years. It was of yore the old coaching house for London'. Seen further down George Street (beyond the cottage), the white building with the low gabled roof is the Little Eastern and adjoining it the Railway Tavern. The building next door is the old Independent Chapel and finally the Golden Lion. Opposite on the right-hand side are the old railway cottages.

Interior, (showing Grape Vines) of the White Hart Hotel, Harwich.

Left: The White Hart also boasted a very fine interior around 1920 and comprised a quadrangle, centrally situated, from which opened the rooms. It is an attractive feature and forms a luxuriously cool lounge furnished with couches in the summer season. It is open to the lofty glass roof, along which the vine is trained, so that in season bunches of grapes hang pendant from the interior of the dome. A gallery runs round the building, midway between the ground floor and the glass roof.

Above: A recent photograph of the Anchor Hotel (now demolished) that had survived the floods of 1953 and was a centre for the close-knit community of Bathside. The hotel was used to hold many functions, as its hall was a popular venue for a great many weddings. It was also the home for the Luney Club formed in 1958, a club that helps elderly residents of Bathside. Since the closure of the Anchor Hotel the club now meets at the Royal British Legion Club to continue their charity work.

Opposite below: Walking across the railway level-crossing brings us into Bathside and the Anchor Hotel, which was trading as a beer-house in 1870 under the auspices of James Spraglin of Ipswich. The Anchor soon became a popular Cobbold house and was the home of the champion quoits team in 1910, the Stour Wanderers, which included six of the Garnett brothers and the captain was lifeboat coxswain Ben Dale, who would call his team together by firing off a maroon. The Anchor had at one time two teams: the Stour Wanderers and the Anchor Rovers and at the 1912 award presentation, the mayor reminded the guests that in the years before having a pitch, quoits was played on Bathside Mud, with Oyster shells used for quoits. 'Champions, the Wanderers, made a great demonstration in the town on Saturday night, when headed by their band and displaying all their cups and trophies won in the quoit arena, they marched through the town, and were given a great reception', reported the local newspaper. The newspaper also reported on 15 September 1894 that a servant Jessie Phipps, aged twenty-five years, was found dead in bed by her mistress, the wife of landlord James Spracklin. It appears the deceased retired to rest in her usual health, after partaking of supper on the previous night. Failing to get a reply when knocking on her door, the deceased was discovered in what Mrs Spracklin thought to be a 'fainting condition'. Stimulants were administered, but to no avail. Dr Evans was called and pronounced her dead.

Above: The Anchor can be seen here as it undergoes demolition to make way for flats in 2004. It had been a popular pub, the only hall in Harwich, and a pub that, had it been restored to its former glory, and had its spacious accommodation converted to modern standards, could still have been a viable proposition.

Left: A menu from The Anchor Hotel's annual dinner, 1930.

An advertisement for The Anchor Hotel from 1962.

Completing the pubs of Harwich, the Three Tuns, as mentioned by Sir James Thornhill in his diary of 1711, stood in a lane off of the old London Road, which is now occupied by commercial premises. Licensed in 1720, but their whereabouts unknown, were the: Three Crowns; Three Mariners; Cock; Stow Boat; Griffin & Crown; Chequers; Rotterdam; Carpenters Arms; Green Dragon; Two Brewers; Coopers Arms and the White Horse, which although shown on a town map of 1825 as being on the same site as the New Bell cannot be correct as the New Bell deeds prove otherwise.

Louisa's Tale of Woe
from contemporary newspaper accounts

Louisa, depicted here entering the pub upright (which is not always how she departed) was described as, 'an inebriate, an incorrigible and degraded woman' born around 1852. Her father was a mariner and she married James, a mariner, the son of a policeman on 29 September 1873. They produced two sons, Charles, born 1874 and James, born 1875 and at that time the family resided in King's Head Street. We first meet up with Louisa in January 1891 when she was brought before the bench for being drunk and disorderly. It was her thirteenth conviction, she was fined 40s and in default of paying, a month's hard labour. She next appeared in June 1900, charged with the same and remanded while arrangements were made for her to be placed in a home for inebriates. Two weeks later the bench was satisfied, in view of her constant intemperance, that it was no use sending her to prison and as certain formalities would have to be made to get her into a home, they would adjourn the case for six weeks. She was bound over to keep the peace in the meantime, but in July she was back again, having been 'of good behaviour until Saturday when she broke out'. The case was adjourned for another month. During November 1905 Louisa appeared again, having been an inmate of the Inebriates Home at Bristol, for being drunk and disorderly, in the case which hd been adjourned in August to see how she behaved. Inspector Lunnis reported the woman had not kept away from drink, though she managed to keep away from his men. Dr Evans said she was incorrigible and it was plain and evident that she could not keep away from drink. He would give her another chance, but she was to understand that if she was convicted of being drunk three times in any year, she would be sent back to the inebriates home, which was the best place for her. Louisa then disappears until July 1906 when she once again is charged for being drunk and disorderly. It appeared that she had just done a term of three years in an inebriates home in Bristol. The sentence was one month's hard labour.

In January 1907 Louisa was living at Assembly Yard, but was back again before the bench. Charged with being drunk and incapable, PC Hills stating that at 9 p.m. on Friday he was in Market Street and saw the defendant in King's Head Street helplessly drunk; too drunk to stand. She was detained until the next morning 'when she was liberated into her own recognisances of £2 to appear before the magistrates'. Inspector Lunnis said that he had made enquiries and found that she had not been served in a public house. She had kept right for three months, when she had a bottle of port wine and a cake sent her for a Christmas box and she had drunk all of the port wine. The magistrates declared it was a very cruel thing to send her away. When she was searched she had £4 in her stockings. Her husband declared he could do nothing with her, the more he tried 'the further he got astern'. He was asked if he treated her properly or do you kick her out of the house: 'I try to get all the liquor away from her' was the reply. He said that 'since she had signed the pledge he was in the habit of giving her money, she sold everything for money, even the food in the house. If she was sent away again it would cost about £1 per week, which he could not afford as he had only spare work.' She was fined 12s or one month's labour. But a week later she was back again, her 32nd appearance, found in Mr Walford's baker's shop too drunk to stand. She was put into the street where she

said, 'policeman I want to go home'. She was locked up. When Louisa was searched a small bottle of whisky was found and 8s 7d in her hand. She had been refused drinks at the Three Cups and Duke of Edinburgh, but said 'they will not serve me in pubs so I send out for it'. She asked to be put under a bond for six or twelve months, and she would keep it. She was fined 9s and 12s costs or one month's labour. She said she would pay it, 'but you only have 8s 7d.' She said she would pay with a sovereign and to the surprise of the female searcher, fumbled in the finger of her glove and found the sovereign. She paid over and was liberated; 'too artful even for the searcher'. At the petty sessions in August 1911, Louisa appeared to an adjourned summons for being drunk. Police Inspector Metcalfe said she had been very good since the adjournment, that she had been no trouble and there had been no complaints. The defendant thanked the bench and said she intended to be good in the future. The magistrate discharged her expressing the hope that she would continue her good conduct. She appeared again in May 1913, charged with being drunk and incapable. PC Walls reported that he saw the defendant fall down twice in Wellington Road. On the road near where she had fallen 4s, a small spirit bottle and her hat were found. The officer reported that she appeared to have lost the use of her legs and wandered in her speech. At the police station she was laughing and crying alternately and claiming that she was not drunk, but had fallen and sprained her ankle. The case was dismissed after adjournment because of her good behaviour in the three months since the case was adjourned. Louisa and James ended their days in Heath House (the workhouse) at Tendring. James died in May 1923 aged eighty, and Louisa passed away in June 1938 aged seventy-six.

The Harwich Brewery

The story of the Harwich Brewery and the links with the Cobbold family is a complex affair; one which is difficult to research due to a number of the Cobbold's records seemingly lost or destroyed. Brewing was certainly taking place in Harwich during the late sixteenth century and quite possibly earlier. Arnold Johnson (brewer) was brewing in 1560 and George Rolfe in 1715, supplying the local beer-houses, merchant and Royal Navy ships. The brewery was on the northern waterfront of the quay, where the Pier Hotel car park now stands. Thomas Cobbold, a maltster from Ipswich arrived in the town in 1723, when the Harwich Brewery was supposedly formed, although there is no evidence of Cobbold coming to Harwich until 1730. It is believed that Thomas Cobbold bought the brewery from Rolfe, who died in 1727, although the Rolfe family were still supplying beer to the corporation in 1736 at a cost of £1 2s per barrel. Due to poor water, described by Thornhill in 1711 as brackish, Cobbold, who, so the story goes, had been bringing water from Ipswich by water schoots (water carrying barges), moved the operation to a new brewery in Ipswich in 1746. In 1752 Thomas I, the maltster, died and Thomas II, the brewer, took over; himself dying in 1767. In 1770 the brewery was leased by Sarah Cobbold, wife of Thomas II, to John Cobbold and Charles Cox, an influential man in Harwich. For fourteen years John had been running the Ipswich operation and Cox the Harwich brewery. This then formed the Cobbold and Cox partnership, which apart from the brewery and inns, ran baths, a bank and were also steam packet agents. Between 1770 and 1790 Cobbold was brewing for HM ships, *Victory* and *Dreadnought*. Each ship had its own brew named after it, which was taken on board each time the ships arrived in Harwich harbour. Thomas (son of John) was the mayor in 1828 and 1843 and had taken over the brewery along with Anthony Cox (son of Charles) at the turn of the nineteenth century. They put the brewery, tun rooms, malt and hop lofts, counting houses and premises, (rebuilt within a few years) together with twenty inns and public houses up for sale by auction and retired in 1840. He died in 1845. The brewery closed, the contents were split up and the site was acquired by John Brice, who built the Pier Hotel. The new brewery now appeared on the site of the old workhouse behind the Three Cups, which John Bull (a member of the Bull family who owned the Three Cups and who used it as a brewery and beer shop) acquired in 1840. This site was to change hands over the years and was acquired by John Cobbold in 1844. He then lost interest and in 1863 it was acquired by John Chevalier Cobbold. The brewery finally closed in 1876 and was demolished to make way for a new vicarage. But the brewing legacy remained with the family as they still owned pubs in the town, and they joined forces with the Tollemache family in 1958 to become Tolly Cobbold. The Harwich Copper (pictured at the Tolly Cobbold Brewery, Ipswich) is believed to be the oldest brewing vessel in existence; however, the date as stated on the plaque of 1723 is in dispute. It is believed that Cobbolds dated the copper at the time they began brewing, although it is thought quite possible that this was acquired from George Rolfe, when they purchased the old brewery, and is thus older than first thought.

Above: Here is an early nineteenth-century print of brewing at home, or possibly at the rear of an inn. When the water was unfit to drink, the brewing process sterilised the liquor making it fit to drink.

Right: A Cobbold advertisement showing the three beers brewed in those far-off days. Presumably the dark stock ale was what we know today as mild.

COBBOLD & CO. LTD.,

Cliff Brewery,

IPSWICH.

❖

The Family of Cobbold have been brewers for over TWO CENTURIES.

The Cliff Brewery in Ipswich was entirely rebuilt in 1894 and equipped with the most modern machinery. They are noted for—

DARK STOCK ALE
LIGHT PALE ALE
AND STOUT

which are brewed under the most hygienic conditions.

❖

WINES AND SPIRITS.

30, Lower Brook Street,

IPSWICH.

A Cobbold advertisement from the 1930s bearing the image of the brewer sampling his own brew. Inset below is the up-dated version used on company notepaper and promotional material today.

·TOLLY·
COBBOLD

Left: Alston's Stour Brewery in the 1920s at Manningtree, from the pen of well-known Great Oakley artist Russell Thomas. Alston's at this time were well known in the Harwich area, owning and supplying many local pubs.

Below: Alston's horse-drawn brewery dray in 1921 delivering to the Green Swan at Stones Green where the storeroom at the side of the pub can be seen. Alston's delivered around four barrels a week to the Swan.

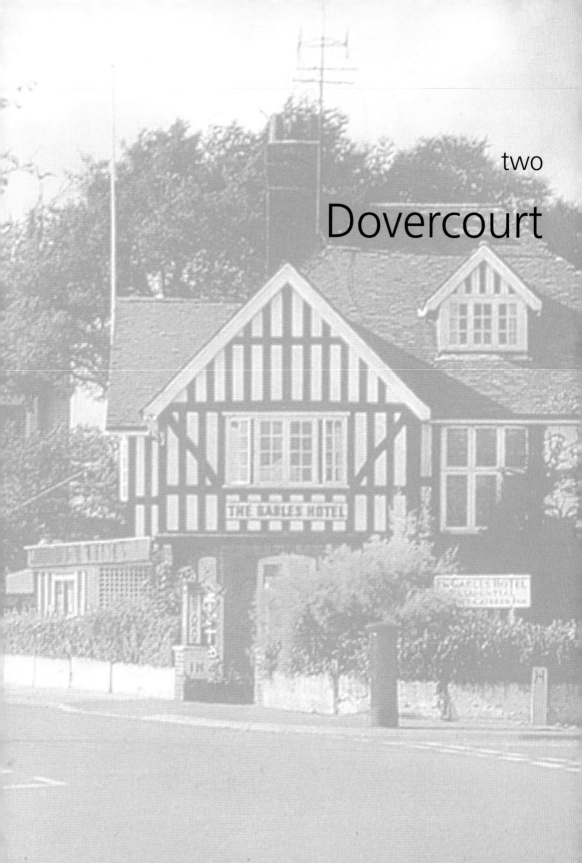

two

Dovercourt

Following the road out of Harwich into Dovercourt, the first port of call was Kettle's, which was not a pub, but was well known for its mineral waters and supplied the majority of the pubs in the area. Starting the business in the cellar of the British Flag, they moved the business to Gywnne Road. Their etched 'Kettles' soda siphons, seen on so many bars, are now becoming collectors' items. The old works closed in the early 1980s and were demolished in 1988; the site is now residential.

Seen here in 1928 are two of Kettle's vehicles and standing by the front van is foreman Jack Mayes and 'Pod' Warren. Two of the men by the other vehicle are Fred Balls and Harry Cooper.

On the opposite side of the road to the King's Arms with the Tolly sign outside is Buckle's the grocers, which was to become Barwell's the off-licence. The shop, along with the adjoining property, was converted to flats in 2004.

An advertisement for Barwell & Sons.

This 1950s photograph shows the King's Arms, which was trading as a coaching inn in 1753, when it was owned by Cobbold, and was a copyhold public house when sold in 1837. The pub contained a spring well, with barley and malt chambers, that supplied the Harwich Brewery.

An advertisement for the King's Arms.

First To-day—and
HAVE IT AT THE
KING'S ARMS HOTEL
The Old Established Firm.

COBBOLD'S FIRST PRIZE PALE ALE and STOUTS.

Wines and Spirits of the finest Quality at Store Prices in half bottles.

D. H. APPLEBY, Proprietor.
Telephone Harwich 100.

HIGH STREET, DOVERCOURT.

Close to Park, Beach & Railway Station.

The oldest Licensed House in the District.

Above: An advertisement for the Kings Arms.

Right: The King's Arms as it is today in its prominent position at the end of Dovercourt High Street.

THE QUEEN'S HOTEL

**HIGH STREET
DOVERCOURT
ESSEX**

Residential
and
Commercial

2 minutes Sea and Station

BARS and RESIDENTS LOUNGE

Rooms available for Socials and Meetings

FULL BOARD or BED AND BREAKFAST

With or without evening meal

**PARTIES CATERED FOR
MODERATE TERMS**

CAR PARK

WRITE
CALL or
PHONE **HARWICH 2634**

Your Host and Hostess
LES & MAY PAYNE

TRUMAN'S BEST BEERS

Left: An advertisement for the Queen's Hotel, Dovercourt, *c.* 1960.

Below: Opposite the King's Arms is the Queen's Hotel in the High Street. It was originally called the Queen's Head Inn, when owned by Robert Dickson in 1859, and was a family and commercial hotel. Owned from 1873 until 1910 by Robert Bagshaw, it became an ale-house owned by Daniel & Co. of West Bergholt and was later to become Truman's.

Turning down Station Road, opposite the railway station, stands the Victoria Hotel. The hotel was known to have been trading in 1861 and was owned in 1873, as an ale-house, by John Wilding. It was later to be owned by Daniel & Co., and later still by Truman Hanbury Buxton. It is said that in the 1920s and '30s, with many hundreds of men employed at Parkeston Quay, the landlord's daughter would go into the upstairs room at knocking off time and look towards Parkeston. When she saw the workers' train departing, she would call down to her dad who would start pulling the pints, so that they were lined up on the bar, ready for when the railway workers walked in. The annual dinner of the staff and platelayers connected with Dovercourt station took place at the Victoria Hotel on 14 February 1895, when a party mustering sixteen sat down. During the evening the usual loyal toasts were honoured, and Messrs W. Cook, F. Borrett, S. Ostler, R. Aldridge, Gill and W. Cook entertained the company with some good songs. The chair was filled by Mr Flowers (stationmaster), while signalman Borrett occupied the vice. The 'Vic' is trading today, although it is up for sale.

Victoria Hotel, ————— OPPOSITE ————— DOVERCOURT STATION

Daniel & Sons' Fine Ales in splendid condition.

Wines and Spirits of the finest quality including all proprietary brands.

Beer, Stouts of all Brands, delivered in dozen and small quantities.

Proprietor ——————————————————— H. J. GOOCH.

An advertisement for the Victoria Hotel.

The Vic today, albeit in need of some tender loving care, still sports the old Truman's signs.

HOTEL ALEXANDRA

3 star A.A., R.A.C. FULLY LICENSED

Near Harwich and Parkeston Quay

Nearest Railway Station, Dovercourt (2 minutes)

40 Bedrooms all with H. and C. running water,
own Water Softening Plant, Central Heating
in Public Rooms, Electric Fires. Lounge,
Reading Room, Billiard Room, Ballroom.
Premier position on the sea front.

Amenities:— Golf, Swimming Pool, Tennis,
Skating Rink, Season Band, Yachting, River
trips to Ipswich, etc.

Garage - 10 cars.

Telephone: Hotel: Harwich 85
                     Visitors: ,,   327
Telegrams: Alexandra, Dovercourt.

PROPRIETORS: VERNON SMITH HOTELS, LTD.

**3 Miles from Parkeston Quay for the Continental Boats.
TRAVEL IN COMFORT AND BREAK YOUR JOURNEY HERE**

An advertisement for the Hotel Alexandra from 1950.

The Alexandra Hotel, Dovercourt Bay

Standing at the top of Kingsway, opposite the Queen Victoria memorial, is the Alexandra Hotel. At a special sitting of the Harwich Licensing Justices in October 1906, the application was made for a provisional licence for the erection of a large residential hotel. It was opposed by Messrs. Cobbold & Co. (owners of the Cliff Hotel), Bullards Ltd (owners of the Phoenix Hotel), Daniel & Son (owners of the Victoria Hotel), Mr Packer (tenant of the Cliff Hotel), Mr Phipps (tenant of the Queen's Hotel), Dick Appleby (tenant of the King's Arms) and the Harwich and Dovercourt Licensed Victuallers Association on the grounds that there were sufficient such places in the town. The hotel was to be built a quarter of a mile from Dovercourt Railway Station, would cost between £10,000 and £12,000 to build and would contain between fifty and sixty bedrooms. In spite of the objections the chairman and magistrates granted the application, feeling that such a hotel was required. The 'Alex' became a popular location as a dance and concert venue. Today the hotel is a Methodist Residential Home.

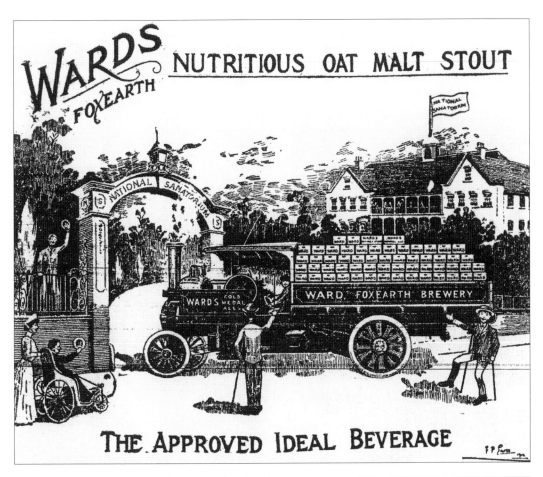

Above: An advertisement from 1912 showing the steam-powered dray of Suffolk brewer Wards delivering to the sanatorium, their Oat Malt Stout a wondrous cure judging by the delight on the faces of the patients.

Right: An advertisement for a town dinner at the Alexandra Hotel in 1927.

A
TOWN
DINNER

Organised by the
HARWICH & DOVERCOURT CHAMBER OF COMMERCE

TO THE

176th HEAVY BATTERY, R.A., (T.A.)
(Local Contingent)

Commanded by Lt.-Col. H. M. A. WARD, D.S.O.

AT THE

HOTEL ALEXANDRA,
on Wednesday, February 2nd, 1927.

BATTERY SUCCESSES in KING'S COMPETITION :

1922		5th Place.
1923		4th Place.
1926		1st Place.

G. CAVE, Esq., Chairman.   F. A. STOOKE, Hon. Sec.

Left: An advertisement for the Gables, *c.* 1950.

Below: Further along Marine Parade the elegant Gables Hotel once stood. Sadly it was demolished and replaced by a block of flats.

Right: An advertisement for the Cliff Hotel from the early 1950s.

Below: The famous white hotel on Dovercourt's Marine Parade is seen here in the 1890s. The Cliff Hotel started life as two houses in the 1850s and shortly after a coffee house was added. From then on it became known as the Cliff Hotel. In the 1870s it was an ale-house owned by Daniels and was taken over by Cobbold at the turn of the twentieth century. In the 1920s it became a Trust House Forté hotel. Since then the 'Cliff' has had various owners, but is still a popular hotel. The hotel remained painted white during the Second World War, as it was used as a navigational aid for British warships entering Harwich harbour.

CLIFF HOTEL
DOVERCOURT

The Cliff Hotel is a comfortable hotel, occupying a commanding position directly facing the sea at Dovercourt. It is well furnished and open throughout the year. Parkeston Quay is $1\frac{1}{2}$ miles from the hotel.

Moderate Tariff   *Telephone Harwich 345*

TRUST HOUSES LIMITED

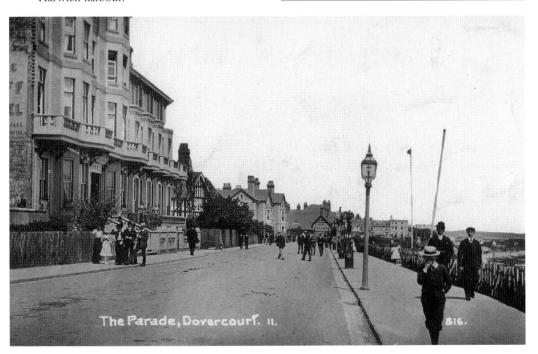

The Parade, Dovercourt. 11.   816.

Strolling down Donkey Hill to Lower Marine Parade, alongside the Retreat opposite the lighthouses is the Phoenix Hotel with its 'Reflections' nightclub. Seen here in 2004 after closure, it is now due to be demolished and replaced by yet more flats.

THE
PHOENIX HOTEL
AND RESTAURANT
LOWER MARINE PARADE
(Fully Licensed)
RESIDENTIAL

MORNING COFFEE   PARTIES
LUNCHEONS CATERED
TEAS FOR

TELEPHONE HARWICH 2071 FOR RESERVATIONS

BULLARDS NORWICH FINE ALES
WATNEYS "RED BARREL" ALES

An advertisement from the Carnival programme of 1962 for the Phoenix Hotel in Lower Marine Parade.

Above: Seen here on the right in this early 1900s photograph (the building with the two chimney stacks) is the first Phoenix Hotel. 'Well known to thousands of visitors in the summer season', the Phoenix Hotel was owned by Bullard of Norwich, under the tenancy of Mr and Mrs Everett and was destroyed by fire in 1914. As reported, 'it was a few minutes after midnight that the outbreak was discovered by Police Sergeant Borrer who noticed smoke while on duty near the Alexandra Hotel. Acting smartly and opportunely he reported the incident and ran to the scene of the fire. Mr and Mrs Everett and their daughters had retired for the night, but the sergeant roused the family who had little time to make their exit and save a few of their more valuable articles. The Phoenix was constructed almost entirely of wood so that the work of destruction was very rapid'. The Phoenix was rebuilt as we know it today and the Everett family took up their tenancy again until 1938 when relatives Arthur and Jo Richards took the hotel until their retirement in 1971.

Right: An advertisement for The Phoenix Hotel from 1950.

The **PHŒNIX HOTEL**
AND
RESTAURANT
(FULLY LICENSED)
LOWER MARINE PARADE
On the sea-front

RESIDENTIAL ALL YEAR ROUND
TERMS 6 GUINEAS (NO EXTRAS)
ILLUSTRATED TARIFF
ON APPLICATION
RESTAURANT OPEN TO NON-RESIDENTS
PARTIES :: RECEPTIONS :: DANCING
Telephones :   Proprietors :
Harwich 71 & 154.   Mr. & Mrs. A. V. Richards.

Next door to the Phoenix Hotel stands the Dovercourt Sports Club. The club came into being through the enterprise of Mr Carylon Hughes. The club is seen photographed here at the time of its completion before it was opened in April 1912. It had tennis courts, snooker room, bar and dining facilities. In 1922 the members agreed to take the premises as tenants of the company and to manage it with their own committee. In 1925 the company sold it to Harwich Corporation. Since then the corporation and now Tendring District Council have owned the premises. In the 1880s the leaseholder Mr Brian Rayner renamed it the Countryman, then in the 1990s Mr John Mowle and Mr Peter Marshall renamed it Squirrels. Now under new licensees, the club remains a vibrant 'members only' club with a popular function hall.

THE ROYAL OAK
(FULLY LICENSED)

MAIN ROAD   -   DOVERCOURT

BED & BREAKFAST - FULL BOARD - MODERATE TERMS - GARDEN FOR CHILDREN

MR. & MRS. D. S. P. HODGSON   **TRUMANS BEERS**

(Lily & Dal)   **Car Park**   Telephone: HARWICH 288

Retracing our steps back to the town and following the Main Road we come to the Royal Oak. The site could possibly have been where the Orange Tree once stood, as it mentioned in John Thornhill's diary of 1711: 'Saturday 2 June, we dined at Ye Orange Tree at Dovercourt'. The Royal Oak, which gave its name to the Royal Oak ground opposite and is the home of Harwich and Parkeston FC, was trading in 1873 as an alehouse owned by Alston the brewer of Manningtree and later became a Daniels, the Truman's house. The pub suffered a fire and was rebuilt by local builders H.H. Bradford. The Royal Oak is trading today as a popular free house, and is well known locally for its good food. This advertisement is from the *Official Holiday Guide to Harwich and Dovercourt, c. 1960.*

Walking up the hill, we pass where the Grapevine once stood. It is shown on the town map of 1874 as adjacent to Blue House Farm. The Grapevine, probably on the site of a vineyard, was owned in 1873 and 1874 by Robert Bagshaw as a beer-house. Further on stands the Royal, built by Cobbold as a replacement for the Royal Hotel in Harwich. It was trading in 1933 and became the headquarters of the Harwich & Dovercourt Homing Pigeon Society and Harwich Rangers FC. Popular Landlord Bill Chambers, who died in 2004, held the pub for many years up until his retirement in 1983.

Just further on, where the health centre now stands, stood the Boatswain's Call. Licensed in 1720 as the Bosun's Call, it was an illicit drinking den often raided by Customs and Excise. It was a black tarred building that was owned (around 1910) by Mr Rowland, whose son worked on the sailing barges and provided the black tar (used for barge hulls) to paint the building. He also supplied barrels of rum. The allotments to the rear of the health centre are still known today as 'Bosun's Call' allotments. Further licensed premises in Dovercourt in 1720, were: Hill House; the Vicarage (where the old Fisher & Woods builders' yard once stood in Lee Road); Cross Keys and the Red Cow.

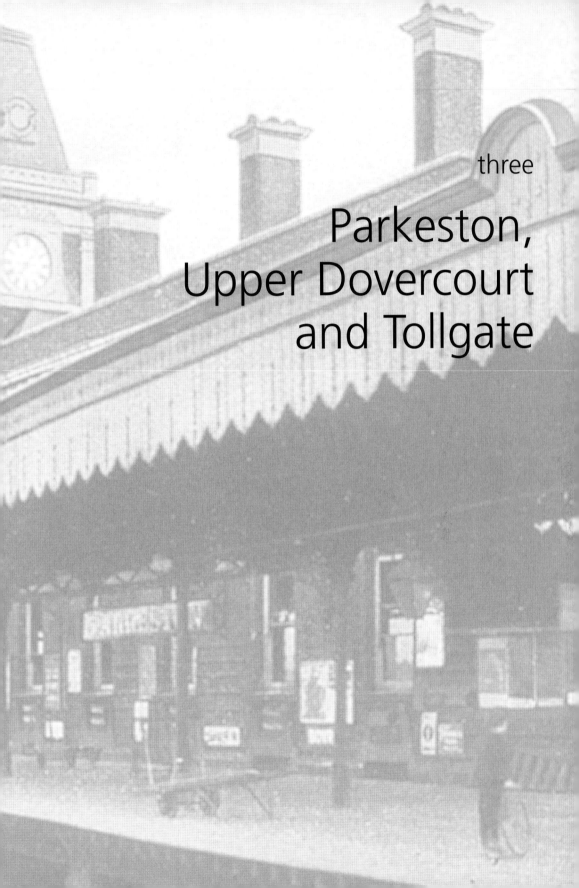

three

Parkeston,
Upper Dovercourt
and Tollgate

Left: An advertisement for the Garland Hotel on Garland Road.

Heading down Parkeston Road towards Parkeston, situated near the gate of Parkeston Cemetery, is Dock Cottage. In later years it was owned by Gladdy Shrive, a well-known accordion player, but prior to that it was a drinking establishment. It was probably more like an off-licence, as in September 1878 a licence to sell beer off the premises was refused because the rateable value of the house (£6) was not sufficient. In 1881 George Osborne applied for an outdoor licence; this was also refused, but in 1882 George Osborne was charged with allowing beer to be drunk on his premises, which meant that his licence only allowed him to sell the same off his premises. He was charged with the same again in 1883. In 1884 he was refused a licence, as his was only temporary until the Parkeston Hotel was finished. The Dock House was created because, prior to land reclamation, the river ran alongside and the Dock House was opened to provide liquid refreshment to those men who worked on the river and land reclamation. Continuing into Parkeston, the Garland Hotel can be seen to the right in this early 1900s photograph taken in Garland Road, which was named after Squire Garland, the Lord of the Manor. The Garland was trading in 1894 as an ale-house owned by Charrington Nicoll, later to be Ind Coope.

The Captain Fryatt seen in Garland Road, Parkeston, in this photograph from 2004. Previously the Garland, this pub was renamed after the well-known local sea captain.

On Parkeston Quay, or as it is known today, Harwich International Port, is the Great Eastern Railway Hotel, which was built in the latter part of the 1800s as part of the new shipping terminal. The hotel closed in 1966 and was converted to port and shipping offices, although the refreshment room and buffet continued to operate.

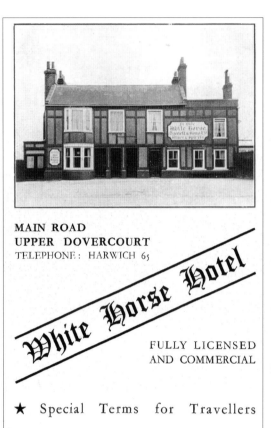

**MAIN ROAD
UPPER DOVERCOURT**
TELEPHONE : HARWICH 65

White Horse Hotel

FULLY LICENSED
AND COMMERCIAL

★ Special Terms for Travellers

Left: An advertisement for the White Horse Hotel, from 1950.

Above: On the Green was the old Bird in Hand that was owned by Charles Cullingham from 1886 until 1914 and was then sold by the Hadleigh Brewing Co. to Mann Crossman and Paulin. The pub was closed in 1938 and is now a private dwelling.

Opposite below: The White Horse at Upper Dovercourt was previously known as the George. It was built on land owned by the Guild of St George, renamed the Great White Horse and was given its present name around the 1870s. This early photograph shows Rose Cottage, now a bookmaker's, alongside it. Owned by Cobbold up until 1837, it was taken over by Samuel Freeman, then Daniels and later Truman's. The White Horse continues to trade today. In May 1817, according to the *Colchester Gazette*, mock elections that followed the official chairing of the Harwich mayor, were held at Dovercourt and it was the occasion for popular festivities. The chairing took place before an immense crowd who had been attracted by the two previous days of amusing sports arranged by Mr Wyllie of the White Horse. The principal amusements were: yawning for a watch chain; smoking for trousers; running for shirts; gingling for hats; jumping in sacks and eating hot hasty pudding. The evening concluded with a ball at the White Horse Inn.

Opposite the old Bird a new Bird in Hand was built around 1936 by Mann's on land known as 'the butts'; land where archers practised. It remained open until 1998 when it was demolished and replaced by a housing association development.

The final throes of the Bird in Hand, another fine pub being destroyed.

"BIRD IN HAND"

Main Road, Upper Dovercourt, Essex
Proprietor: Mr. W. H. RAVEN

MANN, CROSSMAN & PAULIN LTD.
LONDON BEERS . . . *Fully Licensed*

Drink a Mann's Beer

An advertisement for the Bird in Hand from 1950.

On the High Road (as it was then known) on the Green stood the Trafalgar Inn, a fourteenth-century coaching inn. The original building on this site is believed to have been destroyed by fire at the time of the Battle of Trafalgar, and the pub name stems from Nelson's famous sea battle. It is also thought that the pub was converted from a row of cottages that once stood there. In the 1950s the landlord, Ben Storer, made dart boards as a pastime.

A slightly later view of the Trafalgar Inn. The 'Traf' was purchased in 2001 by Ridley's the brewers, and remains the popular pub it has been over many years.

The Trafalgar today with the Upper Dovercourt Methodist Chapel alongside it from which, in 1893, an altercation took place. The newspaper reported that Alfred Hayhoe, a licensed hackney carriage driver, was charged with assaulting Mr Molloy. Mr Molloy stated he was speaking at a Temperance meeting outside the Primitive Methodist Chapel. The defendant came out of the inn and called out in a jeering tone, which broke up the meeting. The complainant was afterwards walking down to Dovercourt when the defendant came up behind him and tried to trip him up. The defendant was very drunk and he was subsequently fined 5s and costs of 16s, or 14 days in jail. The money was paid.

Right: An advertisement for the Devonshire Arms from 1950.

Below: The Devonshire Arms at Tollgate was built where an AA box once stood on the junction of the Main Road and Clacton Road and is seen here in a recent photograph, before it was restored and renamed the Devon in 2000.

MR. & MRS. A. E. BYE

HOST AND HOSTESS AT THE

DEVONSHIRE ARMS

UPPER DOVERCOURT

Invite Your Patronage At Dovercourt's Newest Hotel - The Last Word in Modern Comfort - Luxurious Lounge - Musical Evenings - Congenial Company

SNACKS A SPECIALITY

SPACIOUS ACCOMMODATION FOR CARS AND COACHES

An advertisement for the Devonshire Arms from *The Standard* newspaper, Saturday 16 April 1938. The accompanying article, entitled 'Dovercourt's New Luxury Hotel', reads:

Dovercourt is fortunate to number among its most recent developments the addition of an outsrtanding example of the modern refreshment house – the Devonshire Arms – delightfully situuated at the junction of the Ramsey and Oakley roads at Tollgate, Upper Dovercourt.

It has been erected by Messrs Cobald & Co. Ltd, the well-known Ipswich brewers, who are pursuing a very progressive policy in their houses throughout the district.

Of particularly pleasing design, admirally suited to the commanding site it occupies, Dovercvourt's newest and most up-to-date hotel has a red, multi-colour brick plinth, with rough-cast finish above. The roof is of handmade sand-faced tiles.

The accomodation consists of a large public bar with two entrances on the Oakley-road frontage, and is panelled internally in oak. The saloon bar is similiar and occupies the Ramsey-road frontage, and here the interior panelling is in Indian silver-grey wood. Between these two bars and facing the corner is the off-sales department, also panelled in oak.

The counters are developed on the circular principle and a fine circular oak cabinet, glazed with Venetian striped mirrors, forms a central feature of the bars.

Ample cellar accomodation is provided under the bars, finished with white enamel walls above black enamel skirtings. There is a cellar hoist for conveying cases direct to the bars above, and the whole cellars are of the most modern pattern, being fitted with a special system of air-ducts to control temperatures.

The saloon bar is fitted with a lift connecting with the kitchen above for the purpose of serving sandwiches, snacks or meals.

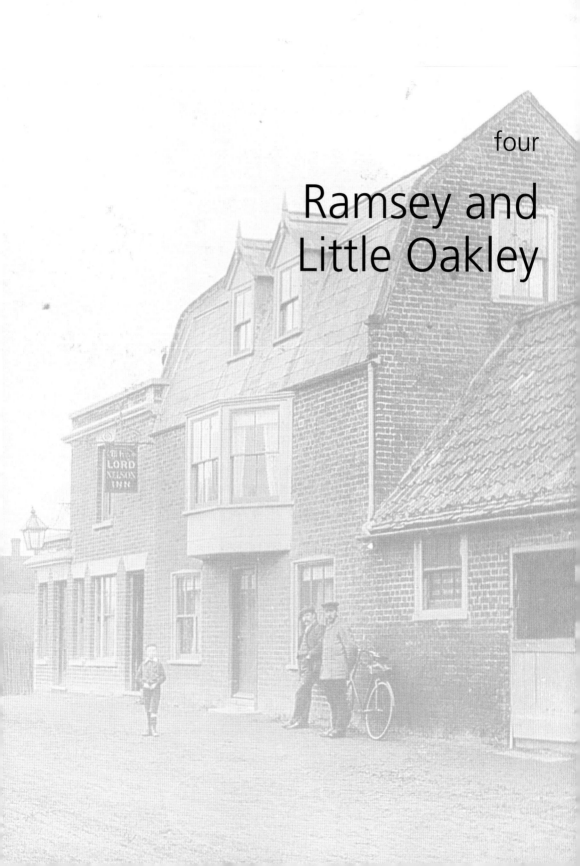

four

Ramsey and
Little Oakley

The Castle Inn, The Street, Ramsey, is a seventeenth-century coaching inn that is still trading today. It traded in 1769 as an ale-house, was sold by Cobbold in 1837 and was taken over by Alston's of Manningtree, later Charrington Nicoll then Daniel & Co., who were then taken over by Truman's. In March 1979 the pub was centre of attention because of the famous 'siege'. A lone gunman held the landlord and his family hostage until police gained control. Landlord Harry Parkin is seen here in 1923 with his family.

The "Castle" Inn,

RAMSEY, ESSEX.

Proprietor: HARRY PARKINS (late of Barking).

Wine and Spirit Merchant. Ales and Stout of the Best Quality, (drawn from the wood).

(Buses to and from Dovercourt pass the door).

Luncheons and Teas provided.
Char-a-banc Parties specially catered for.

"Castle Lodge R A.O.B. meet here every Monday at 7 p.m.
Visiting Brothers will receive a hearty welcome.

An advertisement for The Castle Inn from 1923.

The Prince of Wales, The Street, Ramsey, was trading in 1894 as a beer-house for Steward Patterson. Later to be known as the Gables, shown here, it then became a shop and is now a private residence. Opposite stands the White Swan, which was previously known as the Feathers and traded from 1769 to 1814 as an ale-house. It was sold by Cobbold at auction in 1837 and is now a private house.

The local villagers can be seen in this photograph gathering outside the Castle in 1905 when Sarah Ellis was the landlady. On the 30 March 1875 it was reported in the newspaper that, 'on Saturday evening last, as two men were leaving the Castle Inn, a little skylarking took place, when one of them, a blacksmith named Samuel King, was thrown down in an unaccountable manner and injured his leg. On the arrival of Dr Evans, it was discovered that the man had suffered a severe dislocation of the ankle, and that one of the bones of the leg was broken. This is the second accident of the kind that has occurred from this practice of skylarking within the last two months.'

On the Wrabness Road in Ramsey stands the Lord Nelson, seen here around 1910. It is believed the original name of the alehouse was the Nelson, later becoming the Nelson Head and finally the Lord Nelson; the name changes taking place while the Ward family were landlords.

This is a fine photograph of the Nelson with Dan Taylor outside with his dogs at a time when Colchester Oyster Festival Stout and Truman's London Ale was being served; evidenced from the sign on the wall. The notice of sale, dated 3 December 1824, shows that the building is known as the Nelson but the whole estate including the 2.5 acres of nursery garden is referred to as the Lord Nelson, and were copyhold of the Manor of Michaelstowe Hall, Ramsey. The public house was sold as 'free from the control of any brewer'. The pub was de-licensed in 1961 and is now a private dwelling. Orchard Close and the market garden were purchased by Tendring District Council for council houses but was then sold to a private developer for housing.

The newspaper reported on 3 July 1886 that Charles Button was accidentally shot in the head in the garden of the Lord Nelson. It appears that he was stacking wood, when James Holden, a gardener, who was shooting birds, not seeing Button at the stack, shot at a blackbird flying in that direction and immediately Button fell. Assistance was at once obtained and he was attended by Dr Evans, who found that his right eye had been destroyed and his head seriously injured. It is believed the unfortunate fellow received almost the whole charge of the gun, as many as 175 shots being found in his right arm from the hand to the elbow.

Little Oakley at one time had two pubs, the Horseshoes, which traded between 1769 and 1826 as an alehouse and is now a private residence, and Ye Olde Cherry Tree which still trades today. Originally a tithe cottage built in the thirteenth century, it became an alehouse in the fourteenth century and changed its name to Cherry Tree in the fifteenth. It is said the pub has a priest's hole dating back to Oliver Cromwell's time. Until 1916 it formed part of the Manor of Little Oakley, and was occupied by copyholders.

Another view of Ye Olde Cherry Tree with a meeting of the Hunt gathering outside.

Ye Olde Cherry Tree, seen here in its present guise, is a regular entrant in CAMRA's *Good Beer Guide*, and has won the CAMRA Colchester and North East Essex Pub of the Year competition on more than one occasion. The 'Cherry' is well known for its food and lovers of real ales. Sadly in 2004 this freehold pub was sold to a pub management company upon the retirement of the landlord.

five

Landlords, Landladies and Customers

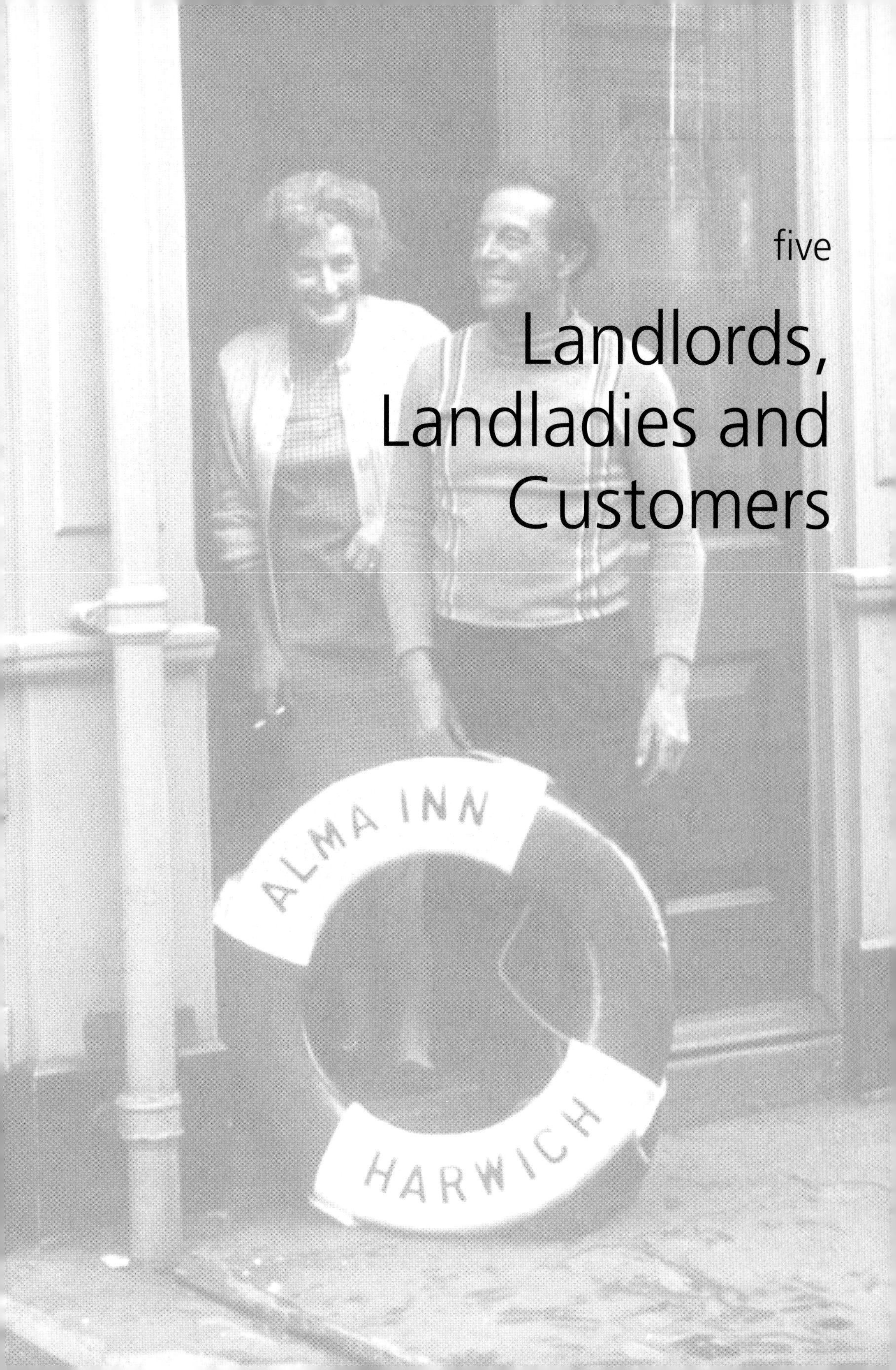

ALMA INN

HARWICH

Landlady Peggy Chambers with Ricky Marsden are seen here outside the Alma during the 1960s.

Brothers Arthur Chambers of the Alma and Bill Chambers of The Royal are seen here checking the deeds in the 1960s.

Arthur Chambers his son Barry and Robin Wallace are seen here rescuing beer from the cellar during the flood that followed heavy rain in 1963.

Bystander Paddy McKenna looks on as the local police check all is well with the residents in the flooded King's Head Street outside the Alma in 1963.

Arthur and Peggy Chambers with Ika Tye and Pony Moore during the 1960s are here admiring the Alma's collection of ships in bottles. Many of these are Lightships made by the Trinity House Light Ship crews; a popular hobby during their time at sea.

Arthur and Peggy Chambers seen in this photograph with the Tolly Cobbold sales rep at their retirement leaving party from the Alma in 1987.

Landladies Mrs Upson, Mrs Proon, Mrs Wink and Mrs Dean are sitting down to lunch in this photograph from around 1950.

Left: The grandparents of Mrs Lydia Whitnall, Mr and Mrs Stevens are photographed here in 1911 with the licensees of the British Flag.

Right: Mr and Mrs Tootell and Mrs Stevens in 1922. They were the parents and grandmother of Mrs Whitnall. Mr and Mrs Tootell took over the British Flag on the retirement of Mr and Mrs Stevens.

Landlord and landlady of the British Flag for fifty years, Claude and Lydia Whitnall are seen here in the 1960s.

British Flag landlord Claude Whitnall is photographed here with barmaid Mrs Pryke in the 1960s.

Left: British Flag landlady Lydia Whitnall.

Below: The retirement of Mrs Lydia Whitnall of the British Flag, in 1984, after fifty years behind the bar. She is seen here with her son and daughters, Linda, Steve, Ann and Christine.

Right: Elsie Smith of the Devonshire Arms is presented with a bouquet by Linda Whitnall, the daughter of Mrs Whitnall of the British Flag, at a Licensed Victuallers' Association function in the 1960s.

With Compliments from

WILL WADE,
NEW BELL,
HARWICH.

Left: This matchbox cover depicts Will Wade, landlord of the New Bell. On the closed edge it says, 'Meet me at the New Bell, Harwich'. The New Bell was noted for 'oyster feasts, stout, wines and spirits of the best quality.'

This 1949 photograph shows Fred and Mabel Dean of the Golden Lion, with Mrs L. Rozier a family friend, Mr Chapman a customer and Frederick Barwood, Mrs Dean's father and landlord of the Foresters Arms.

This photograph was taken in front of the Golden Lion around 1949 and shows Mabel Dean, landlady of the pub, with G. Bond, D. Bond. R. Harris and A. Hunter.

Above: Fred and Mabel Dean, with Fred
Barwood at the darts dinner in the tap
room of the Golden Lion, *c.* 1949.

Right: Fred Barwood in the back yard of
the Foresters Arms. He was landlord there
from 1925 until its closure during the
Second World War.

This family photograph taken at the rear of the Hanover Inn, during the 1920s, is of landlord Fred Hockley and his wife Mabel, sons Fred and Stan and daughter Olive. Fred was originally messman on HMS *Ganges* where he catered for King George V who paid a visit during the First World War. He also established the Blenheim and the Buffs Lodge. His wife Mabel began the Bohemian Society, which was a fairly new 'ladies only' club that met at the Hanover. Their son Fred was best known locally as a winger for the 'Shrimpers', Harwich and Parkeston FC.

A. H. HOCKLEY

Late Messman Royal Navy,

THE HANOVER INN & DINING ROOMS,

Good Beds and Every Accommodation.

CHURCH STREET, HARWICH

An advertisement for the Hanover in Church Street.

Right: Mr Lodge, the last landlord of the King's Head, is seen here in this 1920s photograph alongside his staff and family.

Below: Harry Taylor was the landlord of the Angel and is seen here around 1928 with his wife and their son Aubrey, who in later years was to become landlord of the King's Arms.

John Smith was the landlord of the Elephant and Castle and is seen here around 1904

Jessie Proon and Bert Keeling in this 1937 photograph behind the bar of the Little Eastern.

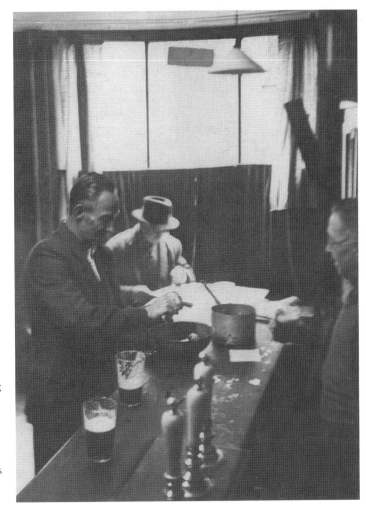

Top: Four men of Harwich, one of whom is believed to be the landlord, Mr Ross, are seen here at the entrance to the Lifeboat Inn during the 1940s.

Right: An interior view of the Lifeboat Inn from the 1940s shows Mr Ross behind the bar – no spirits only beer served in this beer-house.

Inside the Lifeboat Inn's small bar, *c.* 1940. It is said the hatch had to be lifted to play darts.

Two of the Lifeboat Inn's regulars pose for the camera while enjoying a pint.

Right: Eddie Baker, landlord of the Wellington Inn, is seen here in 1958. Eddie moved to the Duke of Kent in Ipswich after leaving the 'Welly'.

Below: Eddie and Kit Baker of the 'Welly' were landlords from 1955 to 1959. After leaving Ipswich they retired back to Harwich.

It's Christmas time around 1958 and Eddie and Kit Baker are with the Christmas raffle prizes.

A rare photograph of Freda Mary Pearce, landlady of the Royal Oak Inn, Dovercourt, in 1932.

six

Champions

The Alma darts champions in the 1950s. Before the camera are, from left to right: Ginger Carrington; Nutty Long; Bertie Good; Alfie Tuffen; Basil Carter; Bert Teatheredge; Len Edwards; Arthur Chambers; Bob Baker; Roy Rumsby; Harold Good; Jimmy Upson.

Darts presentation trophies are laid out at the Royal in the 1960s. Among those present are: Bill Chambers, landlord of the Royal; Sid Simmons; Alfie Tuffen; Peter Collins, from the Skinners Arms, Manningtree, and Bill Bleakley.

The Spread Eagle C Division darts champions 1971 seen here from left to right: Danny Powell; Ivan Hammond; Graham Turner; George Green; Bert Turner; Paddy ?; Alan Howard; Keith Tyrell; Alec McLaughlin; Charlie Leggett and Maurice Hinks. The following season the Spread Eagle had closed and the darts team moved to the Wheatsheaf.

The Alma were many times darts champions and line up again before the camera after the presentation in the garden of the Anchor, *c.* 1955. The team members are, from left to right: Jock Crannagan; Frank Pells; Roy Bridges; Bob Baker; Alfie Tuffen; Bertie Good; Arthur Chambers; Len Edwards; Teddy Bond; Bert Teatheredge; Charlie Long; Harold Good; Roy Rumsby; and Basil Carter.

Regulars from the Little Eastern are seen here in the early 1900s at what looks like a musical evening. The chap in the front row has his accordion ready to strike up a tune.

The 'hairy quoits club' – the name obvious judging by the be-whiskered gentlemen. These men are from the Lifeboat Inn, *c.* 1900.

Dated 1919, these are the men of the Trafalgar Inn steel quoits team. The landlord of the pub in those days was Arthur Welham.

The Trafalgar quoits team, *c.* 1925.

A steel quoits team are seen in this photograph visiting the Castle Inn, Ramsey, in 1912. It is believed this was a visiting team of Harwich seamen. The landlord of the Castle was George Hood. Mr Whiting the local fishmonger is standing at the door. Mr Whiting had a hook instead of a right hand.

seven

Didn't We Have a Lovely Time?

The Stour Wanderers Prize Band, seen here in 1898, were a band who entertained in local pubs. The musician sitting in the centre of the front row is Ben Dale.

The Alma Games Club outing to Great Yarmouth in 1949. Among those ready for the off are: Mrs Hendrick; Mrs Carter; Jackie Upson; Mrs Chambers; Mrs Oakley; Bert Teatheredge; Lil Ridgeon; Harold Good; Arthur Moonie; Mr Chambers; Len Edwards; Mr Scott; Arthur Chambers; Jack Howard; Mrs Bee and Jimmy Upson.

A tradition among Harwich darts teams was the annual outing to Great Yarmouth. This photograph shows the Alma Games Club before their coach trip in 1950.

The Alma Club ready for their outing to Great Yarmouth in 1951.

Bert Turner, Graham Turner, Ivan Hammond, Brian Hastings and Mr Clarke are celebrating the
Spread Eagle winning the C Division darts championship in 1971.

It's summer carnival time in the late 1950s and the float from the Alma, the 'Alma Fillys', shows,
from left to right: Arthur Chambers; Roy Bridges; Joe Newbiggin; Bob Baker and Billy Good. It
looks like Joe is playing the string tea chest bass. The story goes that the barrel fell off the float half
way round the procession route and shook the beer up a bit!

The Rising Larks clog dancing team seen performing outside the New Bell in 1983.

'All aboard' for a pub outing from the Victoria Hotel in one of Starling's first coaches. The driver was Bill Lofts.

The Smith family, friends and regulars from the New Bell in the 1920s off for a day out in a charabanc.

A shiny charabanc with a gleaming bell ready for the off to Clacton in July 1924 with regulars from Ye Olde Cherry Tree, Little Oakley.

Above: Sitting down to Christmas dinner in the 1960s at the Alma are, from left to right: Mrs Carrington; Billy Barker; Mrs Coombes; –?– ; Mrs Ward; Bert Teatheredge; Mr Finningham; Charlie Boot; Billy Good; and Bob Scott.

Right: Albert Miller, Nunc Smith, and Bob Scott are seen here enjoying their Christmas meal at the Alma in the 1960s.

Dan Taylor with his dogs, waiting for opening time outside the Lord Nelson in Ramsey in the 1920s.

A national advertising campaign to promote beer from the 1930s..

Other local titles published by Tempus

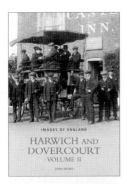

Harwich and Dovercourt Volume II
JOHN MOWLE

Illustrated with over 200 archive images, this collection documents many of the major changes and events that have taken place over the last century in Harwich, Dovercourt and surrounding villages, including Mistley, Parkeston, Ramsey, and Little and Great Oakley. The selection records shops and businesses, pubs and hotels, schools and churches, and the people who lived and worked in the area.
0 7524 3084 X

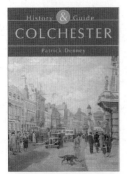

Colchester History & Guide
PATRICK DENNEY

Once regarded as the capital of Roman Britain, the town of Colchester has witnessed many events during its long history. This book traces its history from early Celtic origins and Roman settlement, through plague and Civil War, Victorian enterprise and social reform, to the growth of industry in the twentieth century. Also included is a walking tour which guides readers to places of historic interest still to be seen in the town centre.
0 7524 3214 1

Southend Voices
FRANCES CLAMP

This book brings together the personal memories of people who have lived and grown up in the seaside town of Southend-on-Sea during the last century. Reminiscences range from childhood games, work and wartime to schools, churches and local characters. Recollections include stories of the Palace Hotel, the Kursaal and the pier. The stories are complemented by over 120 photographs drawn from the contributors' own collections.
0 7524 3215 X

Speedway in East Anglia
NORMAN JACOBS

Containing 200 illustrations, this volume covers the history of speedway in the region from its beginnings on the grass track at the First Stadium in Norwich in 1930 up to the present day. It also features histories of all the local teams, including Norwich, Ipswich, Yarmouth, King's Lynn, Rayleigh, Peterborough and Mildenhall, and describes the many star riders associated with East Anglia, including Bert Spencer, Aub Lawson and Ove Fundin.
0 7524 1882 3

If you are interested in purchasing other books published by Tempus, or in case you have difficulty finding any Tempus books in your local bookshop, you can also place orders directly through our website

www.tempus-publishing.com